Here Is Your Hobby: DOLL COLLECTING

Doll collecting is a hobby which invites the reader to enjoy a lifetime of satisfaction from dolls, rather than discarding these "playmates" of childhood. The author treats of the history of dollmaking and imparts some knowledge of other countries and the cultures of other centuries. The reader learns how to make dolls, how to repair broken dolls and how to organize and display her collection.

HERE
IS
YOUR
HOBBY:

Doll Collecting

By
Helen
Young

G. P. Putnam's Sons   New York

Titles in the HERE IS YOUR HOBBY series are:

ARCHERY
ART
CERAMICS
DOLL COLLECTING
FISHING
SCIENCE EQUIPMENT
STAMP COLLECTING

Third Impression

© 1964 by Helen G. Young

All Rights Reserved

Published simultaneously in the Dominion of
Canada by Longmans Canada Limited, Toronto

Library of Congress Catalog Card Number: 64-14217

MANUFACTURED IN THE UNITED STATES OF AMERICA

10214

ACKNOWLEDGMENT

Grateful acknowledgment is made to Ruby Short McKim, who first inspired the author to make and collect dolls, and to the owners of many of the dolls shown in this book — Blanche Adams, Miriam Benton, Jan Chamlee, Dorothy Mathis, and Lori Silverwood.

To the Chamlee girls,
Ann, Rebecca, Marta Helen, Gabrielle

CONTENTS

1

Why Collect Dolls?

Have you ever wondered what will happen to your dolls after you decide you are "too old to play" with them? You probably will not wish to throw them away, so you may decide the best answer is to become a doll collector. Collecting dolls is just another way of playing with them for the rest of your life.

Collections are fun in unexpected ways, and that certainly applies to doll collecting. For example, you will make new and interesting friends of all ages, with the love of dolls tying you together. There's no age limit to being a doll collector.

From your collection you will learn fascinating things about history, costumes, geography, art, ceramics, current events, textiles, books, and faraway people and places.

There are several ways to start a doll collection, but the easiest way is to begin with the dolls you already have, then add others. Perhaps your most precious doll is a bisque one, like Alicia Patricia Patty Alice, the first doll in my own collection, who was waiting for me under a Christmas tree a long time ago. She wears the same blue sailor dress she wore then, the same lace-trimmed underwear. Her wig was made of the blond hair saved when her "mother" gave up pigtails. She smiles, showing four little white teeth, and her blue-glass eyes twinkle, as if she were thinking, "You learned to sew by making my clothes," and I whisper, "You're right, but I wasn't supposed to know that. It was your grandmother's idea."

Or your oldest doll may be a Bye-lo, one of the most famous babies of all time. You love her because she looks exactly like a new baby. Grace Story Putnam, the famous sculptor who designed her, used a three-day-old baby as a model.

Although you will be tempted to keep every doll that comes your way, remember: It isn't the size of a collection that's important, but rather that each doll in it means something. There are a great many kinds of dolls, and a wise collector tries to include one example of each kind in her collection. This could mean that your goal would be to own one wooden doll, one made of wax, one of fine china, one of pink bisque, one of cloth, and one of each of the odd materials like corn husks, leather, dried apples, shells, plaster, and even dough. In later chapters, I'll tell you how to make some of these dolls for yourself.

Dolls are made in every country in the world, and some collectors limit their collections to foreign dolls. Their relatives and friends who travel need never have any doubt about what souvenir to bring home to such a doll collector.

Or you can collect or dress dolls to represent each one of our states: a hillbilly, a Texas Ranger, a northwoods lumberjack, a hula dancer, a Navajo Indian, a Pennsylvania Dutch child.

You can dress your dolls in scraps of material from your own dresses, copying the styles. Then, when your collection is old, you or your daughter or granddaughter will laugh at the funny way girls dressed, back in the "old days."

Paper dolls are fun. Collect ready-made movie-star paper dolls, or make your own and draw and paint clothes for them. As a result, you may discover that you have a real talent for dress designing and decide to become a fashion artist.

These are just a few suggestions. There are many other ways to enjoy doll collecting.

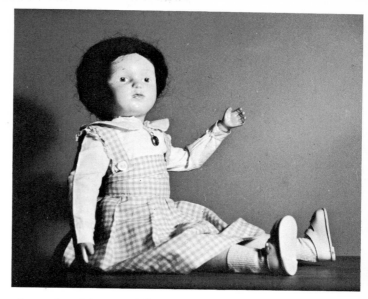

A wooden Schoenut doll waves to doll collectors. She and original clothes are in perfect condition. She's unbreakable, has steel spring joints, and was made about 1915.

Unless you have a large place to display your dolls, it is best to limit their height to not more than 10 inches. If your favorite doll is a large one, she can be an exception, and perhaps sit in her own rocking chair in the corner of your bedroom.

It may be a long time before you have to go out and buy dolls for your collection, because once your friends discover what you are doing, they will shower you with dolls, old and new.

Never pass a thrift shop without looking in the bin holding dolls waiting for repairs. They may be old and dirty and broken, but often need only a thorough cleaning and a few repairs to turn them into real beauties. You can practice working on a few of these orphans and eventually may be asked to repair dolls for other collectors. This is a good way to earn money. In a later chapter, you'll see how a sad and ugly Mexican doll was turned into a dazzling beauty, at almost no cost.

When you wander through toy stores, do you ever think, "What next! Dolls talk and walk and drink. There can't be anything new!" But in the past, there have been stranger dolls than these. Years ago there were life-sized dolls made especially for use in training nurses to bandage and care for sick people; dolls once carried medicine and secret messages in wartime; and for a long time, Paris dressmakers sent dolls to other countries to model grown-up clothes. It was Rose O'Neill's Kewpie doll that made its designer rich and famous. It was Emma Clear's skill in repairing old dolls that turned an isolated chicken ranch into the Humpty Dumpty, the most wonderful doll hospital in the world.

Suppose you have only one doll. She may be rare and lovely, old or new, made in the United States, Europe, or Asia; or she may be an inexpensive doll from the dime store. On the other hand, she may be a doll you have made. With this one doll, you can still make doll collecting your hobby. Make clothes for her, or hats (hats are so quick and easy to make). Use bits of cloth and lace and your own imagination. Dress her in the national costumes of each country in the United Nations, or for every period in history. You will find pictures in books and magazines in schools and libraries.

Later, we will talk about dressing dolls and about making patterns for their clothes. Becoming a doll dressmaker is another way to earn money.

But above all, dolls are made to be loved.

2

Rags Come First

One of the oldest toys in the world is a cloth doll stuffed with papyrus which belonged to a Roman child who lived 300 years before the time of Christ. It is the only one of its kind and is now in a museum.

A cloth doll is a rag doll. So, as you see, the story of rag dolls begins far back in history. There are countless younger, less valuable rag dolls in many museums, pictured in books, and on the shelves of fortunate collectors. And many rag dolls are being made today.

Our pioneer ancestors were forced to make much from very little, and their rag dolls are good examples of how resourceful they were. Some of the earliest American dolls belonged to children of Pilgrims, and some crossed the continent in covered wagons. One of these, little Abby, was made from a scrap of homespun cloth. Her hair is a handful of unspun wool, and her features are marked with berry juice. Her clothes are of the simplest style — a square of cloth with holes cut in it for head and arms. She is now faded and flat, but a priceless treasure, for

Curly-haired rag doll in colonial costume, and a modern child doll, show how similar materials can be made into dolls that look different. *Courtesy of Blanche Adams.*

while there are hundreds of dolls just as old, there is only one little Abby.

Years passed, but rag dolls continued to be made only at home. You can sometimes find one of these old rag dolls that was made by hand, before the invention of the sewing machine, but they are rare. The only way to judge a rag doll's age is by the kind of material used for the body and the clothes. If you have inherited a homemade rag doll from your mother or grandmother, be sure to give her an honored place in your collection.

During the 1800's, manufacturers entered the rag-doll business, and most commercial cloth dolls made between that time and World War I were given as premiums with flour, soap or coffee. These advertising dolls were stamped or printed on cloth in natural colors. Directions for cutting out, sewing and stuffing them were included. Some of the most popular of these were the Aunt Jemima Mammies, Palmer Cox Brownies, Cream of Wheat Rastus, Sunny Jim ("Force Made Him Sunny Jim," the cereal claimed), Buster Brown, and Puffy (Quaker Oats). Girls in

1900 probably exchanged a Brownie for a Rastus, or a Puffy for an Aunt Jemima, just as today's young people trade the plastic and cardboard toys packaged with cereals.

It was also during this time that hundreds of patents for rag dolls were registered in the Patent Office, Washington, D.C. There are far too many to list here, but a few of the favorites were Rose O'Neill's stockinet Kewpies, about 1909; the Kathe Kruse dolls, first exhibited in 1912; Raggedy Ann and Andy, from the Johnny Gruelle books, in 1919; and the beautiful Lenci felt and pressed-cloth dolls, patented in 1921.

But the homemade rag dolls were still the most interesting, just as they are today. Your own first doll was probably a rag baby, for children always love these soft, cuddly, unbreakable toys. Trying to list or even describe all the ways for making them is as impossible as trying to picture every little girl in the world. For every rag doll made at home is original, unlike any other doll made by the same pattern, of the same materials. The dolls

English-made golliwog doll has felt clothes of red, yellow, purple. Golliwogs were introduced in story by Bertha and Florence Upton, "The Adventures of Two Dutch Dolls and a Golliwog," still popular in America, England.

I make cannot duplicate the ones you make, for we each put a touch of our own individuality into everything we construct.

The making of rag dolls is a wonderful way to add to or even begin your doll collection, for the materials are inexpensive and easy to find, and they are simple to work with. You can limit the dolls you make to one size, one country or one period. You can make only girl dolls or boy dolls, women dolls or men dolls. You can vary sizes, from life-sized to dollhouse-sized and even smaller.

The dolls you make may be the simplest kind of all, cut from a cotton sock and stuffed with cotton. Or they may have cloth bodies stuffed with sawdust. You may cut the bodies in one piece or have separate, movable arms and legs. Or the rag bodies may have either rag heads or those made of china, papier mâché or wood. Dolls may be washable for babies to play with, or teen-agers for you to dress in sportswear or formals. They may be modernistic mannequins or costume or character dolls.

Collectors' dolls are often a standard size, 8 to 9 inches tall, and they may be dressed in costumes representing characters in books or plays, in the native dress of other countries, or in clothes of your own country. Using the same pattern, make the body of flesh color for Caucasians, tan for Indians and Orientals, and brown for Negroes. Change the hair color or style, making red curls or black crew cuts, bangs or braids. You don't need a separate pattern for each doll.

Since the proportions and features of human beings are the basic measurements for a doll, here are a few rules to guide you when you design a doll. Use the length of the head from the top of the head to the tip of the chin as your unit of measurement.

1-year-old baby is	4	heads high
3-year-old child is	5	heads high
5-year-old child is	6	heads high
10-year-old child is	7	heads high
15-year-old child is	7½	heads high
Adult is	8	heads high

Let's make a pattern for a woman doll, using this formula as a

16

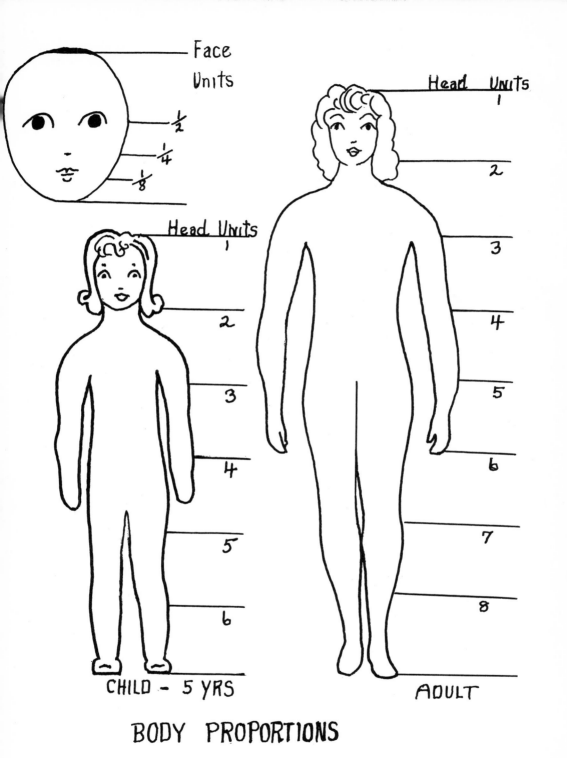

Face
Units

Head Units

½
¼
⅛

Head Units
1
2
3
4
5
6
7
8

Head Units
1
2
3
4
5
6

CHILD - 5 YRS

ADULT

BODY PROPORTIONS

These face and body proportions are basic guides in designing all dolls.

guide and checking our drawing with the chart in the illustration as we proceed.

On a sheet of paper, using pencil and ruler, draw a vertical line 8 inches long. One inch from the top of this center line (⅛ of the total length), mark a short cross line. This locates the tip of the chin.

Now, following the illustration, sketch in the rest of the figure. Note that the armpits are 2 head units below the top of the head; the fingertips are about halfway between the crotch and the knees; the knees are about halfway between the crotch and the feet. The width of the body at the shoulders is a trifle more than 2 head units.

As you sketch the figure, try to keep each side of the outline an equal distance from the center line. Fold the paper along the center line, and cut through both thicknesses at the same time. Unfold the doll you have just cut, and check it again with the chart to make sure its proportions are still correct. Trim or change the pattern until they are. This gives you a basic pattern for a doll body.

In order to know where to place the features on the face, consult the diagram that shows their basic locations. An imaginary line drawn through the eyes will be halfway between the top of the head and the tip of the chin. The nostrils are halfway between the eyes and the tip of the chin. The mouth is halfway between the nostrils and the tip of the chin. The eyes are one eye length apart.

In the accompanying pages you will find patterns for making four kinds of rag dolls. On some of them you'll notice that the paper is ruled off into squares, in the scale of one square to one inch. This is to help you copy the pattern accurately. Here's how you do it: Measure a sheet of paper carefully and mark it off into 1-inch squares. Now draw in the outline of the pattern, repeating what you see in the book. It is easiest to do this if you begin at the upper left hand corner of the paper, using the cross lines to guide you. Work carefully, so that your pattern will be exactly like the illustration.

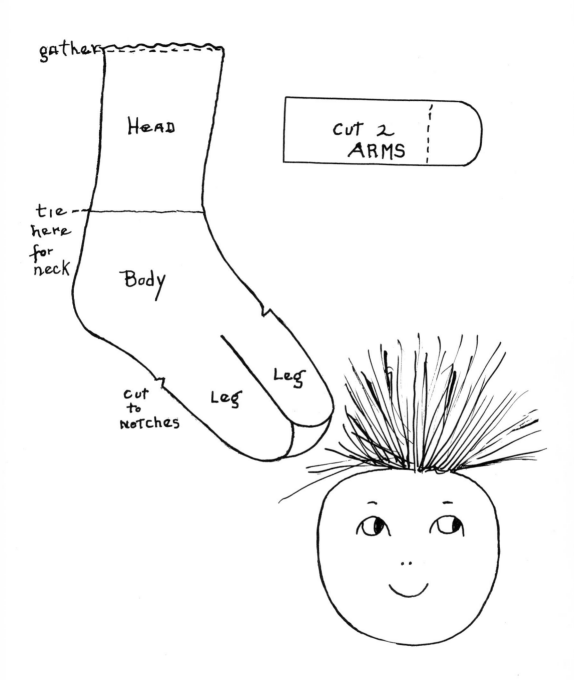

gather

HeaD

cut 2
ARMS

tie
here
for
neck

Body

cut
to
Notches

Leg

Leg

Cut cotton sock as shown, then spread it flat and sew legs together. Cut
pieces for arms from other sock of pair. Stuff arms and sew them onto
body after it's stuffed. Make yarn tassel and fasten to top of head. Press
ends down. Doll may be dressed but is complete without clothes.

Trace this pattern onto a piece of thin cardboard (about the weight of a filing card) and cut out each piece, marking it as you go. Place each pattern in an envelope, and mark it with the name and size. This will give you a strong, durable pattern that will be usable for making many dolls.

If you wish to make a doll either larger or smaller than the patterns shown here, simply increase or decrease the size of the squares on your drawing. For example, if you want a doll that is only 7½ inches high, rule the sheet of paper into ½-inch squares instead of 1-inch squares and proceed as you did with the larger doll. Or, to double the size of the doll patterns, work with 2-inch squares.

This is a good place to mention a rule for the making and dressing of all dolls, as well as for all handiwork: Draw, cut, measure, and sew exactly and without trying to hurry. Follow each step carefully and as perfectly as possible. If a doll is worth making, it is worth good workmanship.

Rag dolls can be made of many different kinds of materials, from felt or Turkish toweling to cotton cloth. Probably the easiest material to use is a firm, fine cotton like percale, sateen or muslin. Flesh pink is a good color to use. For some foreign dolls, make the bodies of light tan or medium brown.

Place the material you have chosen on a table and smooth out all wrinkles. Now pin the pattern pieces onto the cloth. Cut around each piece close to the pattern, by making neat little snips of the scissors so there will be no ragged edges.

Pin the matching pieces together *wrong side out* and baste them together. Sew the seams about ⅛ of an inch from the edge, taking small, even back stitches. See the illustration for the way to make back stitches. If you have never tried to use a thimble when you sew, this is a good time to begin. Doll collectors should be good dressmakers, and good dressmakers wear thimbles. A thimble may seem awkward at first, but you will soon discover that sewing goes faster when you wear one, and you won't keep gouging your finger with the needle. Be sure to leave an opening somewhere on each piece of the body for inserting the stuffing later on.

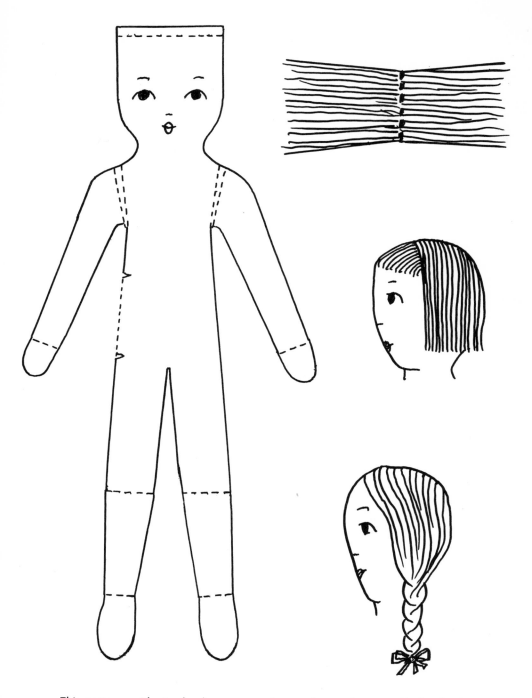

This pattern, with simple changes, can be used to make more kinds of dolls than can any other. In this size, it's ideal for collectors. Dotted lines are small running stitches. Begin stuffing at feet, stuff to dotted line, make stitches, and so on. After stuffing, sew beween notches.

Turn the pieces right side out after making the seams. Now stuff each part firmly with either fine sawdust, kapok or cotton. Sawdust may be obtained free from a lumber yard or a carpenter's workbench. Before using it, sift it through a coarse sieve to remove splinters and scraps of wood. Kapok is a filling material made of cottonlike fibers. Both kapok and cotton are inexpensive and may be bought in all yardage and variety stores. If you use cotton, pull it into small bits and pack into place smoothly, so there will be no ugly bumps on the doll. Use your fingers to pack the stuffing firmly, or press it in place with the handle of a wooden spoon, working it down as you go rather than waiting until the entire body is filled.

Begin the stuffing by filling the doll's feet. When the foot is firmly stuffed, bend the leg at the ankle and catch the cloth together at the fold with an invisible stitch, to hold the foot at right angles to the leg. Then continue stuffing the leg. Stuff the body, but before you start to fill the head, wrap cotton around a stick the length of half a lead pencil and insert the wrapped stick into the body, allowing it to extend halfway up into the head. Complete the stuffing of the head. This stiffened neck will keep the head from flopping.

Turn in the cloth edge at the top of the head and also turn in the openings you left in the seams for inserting the stuffing. Sew the edges together with tiny overcasting stitches. The seam at the top of the head will be covered by the wig.

If you are going to indicate fingers and toes, do this next by taking small running stitches completely through the stuffing and both thicknesses of cloth. Fasten the end of the thread securely and run the end of thread up into the body to hide it.

When the head, arms or legs are made separately before being joined to the body, use two strands of heavy thread for the overcasting used to join them. Fasten it securely. This is important, as a doll is often carried by the arm or leg.

In making small dolls, it is sometimes easier to turn in the edges of the pieces and overcast them together on the right side, instead of seaming them on the wrong side. Sewing on the right

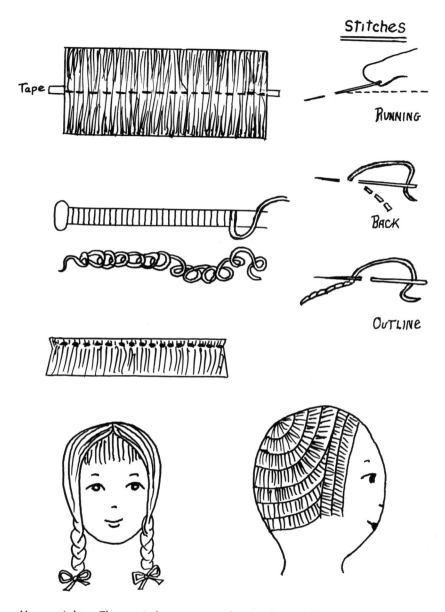

Stitches

RUNNING

BACK

OUTLINE

Tape

Upper right — Three stitches most used in making dolls. Upper left —
Wind cardboard strip with yarn or embroidery floss. Insert strip of nar-
row cotton tape as shown, make back stitches through yarn and tape,
for parting hair. Wind yarn around large knitting needle. Dampen
thoroughly. When dry, remove from needle. Make as many ringlets as
needed to cover head. Make fringe as shown in top drawing, but cut it
close to parting line on one edge. Sew in place as shown at lower right.
Pigtails are made as shown at upper left, using wide cardboard strip so
strands are long enough to braid. Sew strips of fringe under it, for bangs.

Close-up of Rusty the clown. His features are embroidered on head, except for nose, which is a circle of red felt cemented in place.

side is always the best way to make felt dolls, but with felt, do not turn in the raw edges.

It is possible to mark the features on the face of the doll before sewing the body together, but I prefer waiting until the doll is assembled before doing this. Mark the features after you fasten on the wig or make the hair.

Choose one of the following ways to mark the features:

1 — Embroider features by outlining with simple outline stitch.

2 — Use a fine brush and indicate the features with tempera paint, oil paint, watercolor, colored ink or crayon.

3 — Sew tiny circles of felt for marking the eyes. Cut a bow-shaped piece of felt for the mouth and sew it in place with invisible stitches.

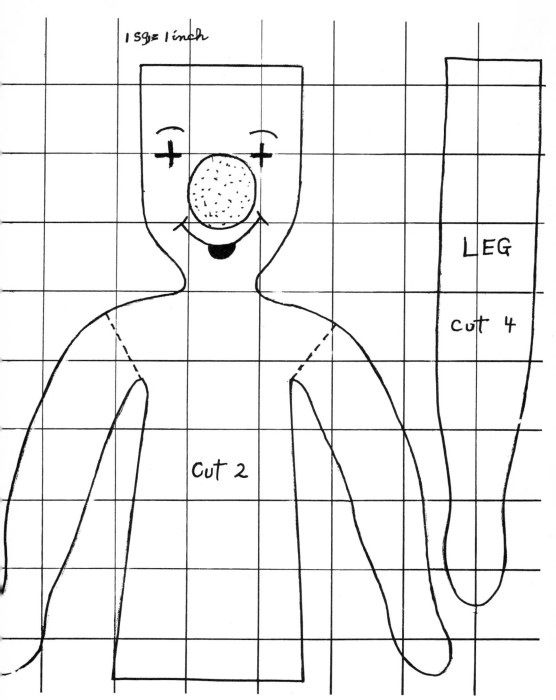

1 sq = 1 inch

LEG

Cut 4

Cut 2

Pattern for body of Rusty the clown. Draw around outline. Add ⅛ inch on all edges for seams. Leave top of head and top of leg open for stuffing, then overcast edges together to close.

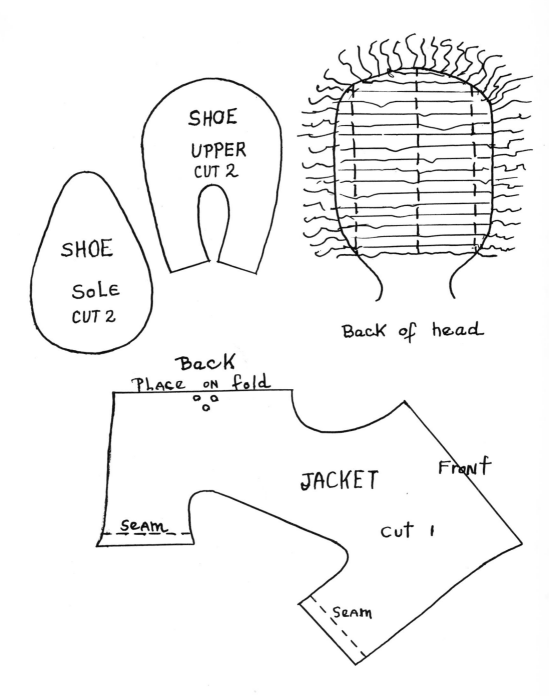

SHOE UPPER
CUT 2

SHOE
SoLe
CUT 2

Back of head

Back
PLACe oN fold

JACKET

Front

SeAm

cut 1

SeAm

Patterns for Rusty's jacket and shoes. Use felt and sew shoes together on right side. His hair is made by tacking lengths of yarn across head with stitches of same color.

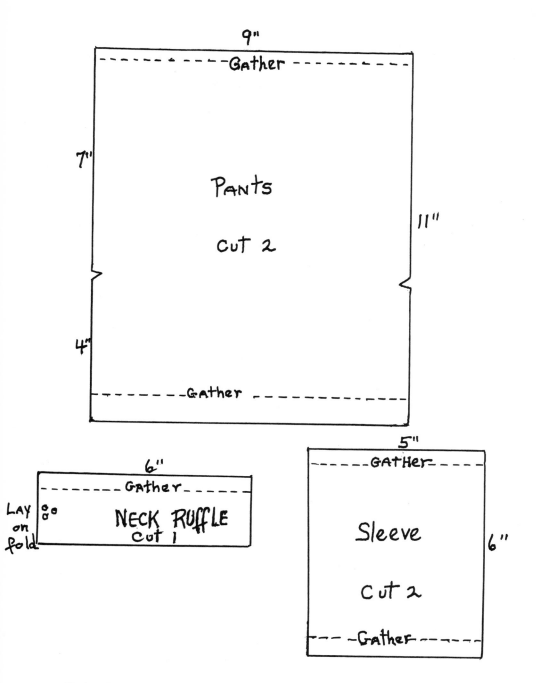

9"

──── Gather ────

7"

PANTS

Cut 2

11"

4"

──── Gather ────

6"

──── Gather ────

LAY
on
fold

NECK RUFFLE
Cut 1

5"

──── GATHer ────

Sleeve

Cut 2

6"

──── Gather ────

Clothes for Rusty are cut as shown. Sew pants pieces together from top edge to notch, then sew each 4-inch-long section together below notch, to make pants legs. Gather top edge and fasten on body just under arms. Make sleeves, tack in place. Cover raw edges with jacket, neck ruffle.

Mary Ann can move her arms and legs. She has perky pigtails and a big smile. The freckles on her nose don't seem to bother her.

4 — Combine one or more of these methods. For example, make the eyes of felt, the eyebrows of outline stitch, the mouth of tempera paint.

5 — Rub a tiny dab of rouge on the cheeks just under the eyes, blending the edges.

The finest dolls never have individual eyelashes marked around the eyes. A simple curved line is more natural looking, with the top of the pupil just touching the top of the curve.

For indicating the nose, two small French knots may be embroidered on the face with pale-pink floss, or you may simply make a short line of the pink floss.

Here are different ways to make the hair:

1 — Remove the wig from some other doll and glue it in place on your rag doll, holding it in place tightly with a head scarf until the glue is dry.

2 — Make a wig in any one of the ways shown in the illustration, using either yarn or embroidery floss.

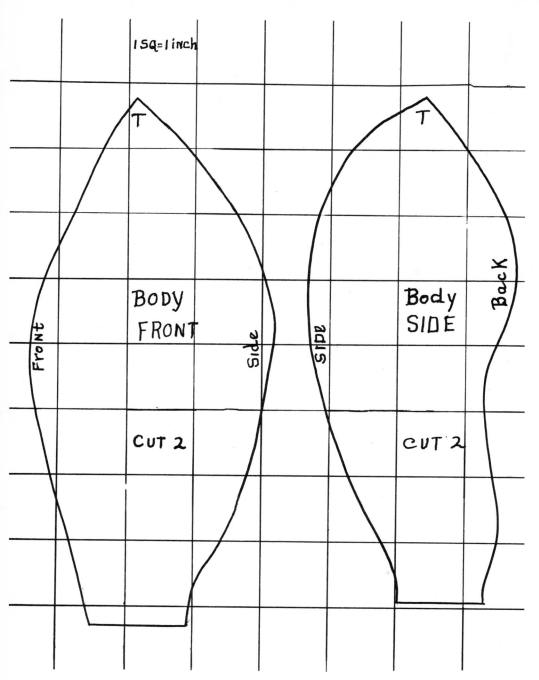

1 Sq = 1 inch

T

Front

BODY
FRONT

Side

CUT 2

T

Side

Body
SIDE

Back

CUT 2

Mary Ann has a body of pink sateen. Cut pattern by following diagram, and sew pieces together, leaving flat edges open for stuffing.

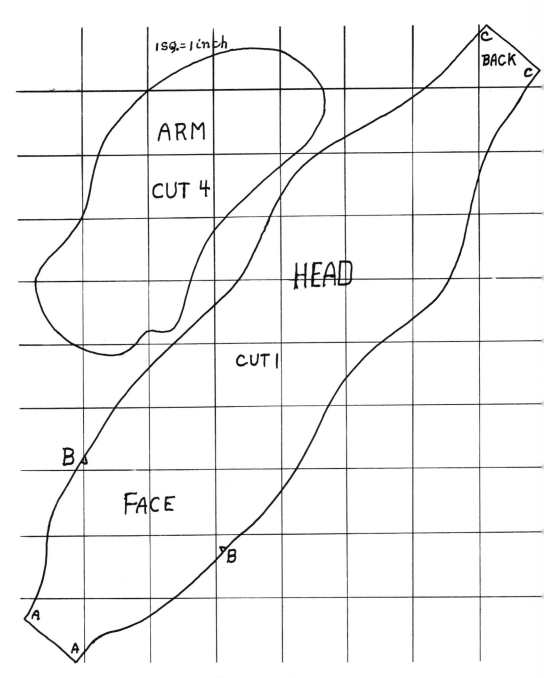

ISq.=1 inch

ARM

CUT 4

HEAD

CUT 1

C
BACK
C

B

FACE

B

A

A

Cut pattern as given on diagram. Sew head piece to side head pieces as lettered. Leave bottom edge open for stuffing. When body is completed, turn under edge of cloth at neck edge of head and sew firmly onto doll body. Sew legs to lower part of body and you've a whole Mary Ann.

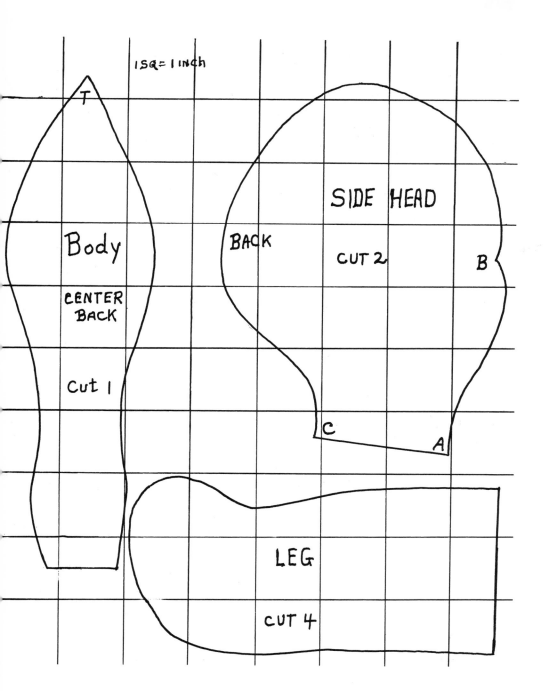

1 SQ = 1 INCH

T

Body

CENTER
BACK

Cut 1

BACK

SIDE HEAD

CUT 2

B

C

A

LEG

CUT 4

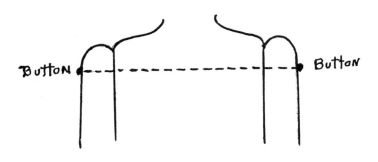

Button ●— — — — — — — — — — — — — —● Button

GATHER

DRESS SKIRT

5½"

HEM

SEAM

36"

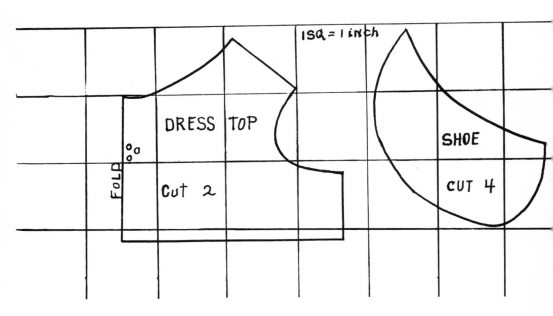

1 SQ = 1 inch

DRESS TOP

SHOE

FOLD

Cut 2

CUT 4

Fasten Mary Ann's arms to body as shown, so the may be moved. Use heavy thread or twine, and an upholstery needle to run it through the body from one button to the other. Fasten invisibly. Make dress of any soft material, the shoes of felt or soft leather.

Mary Ann's faces may be varied further by changing hair color or shape of mouth, nose, eyes. Use one of these for big rag doll, or follow your own ideas. Boy dolls can have same features, different hair styles.

3 — Take long stitches through the cloth of the doll head to represent hair. This is a good method to use on dolls intended for babies and small children, as it is washable and cannot be pulled out.

4 — Make a wig of artificial hair, obtained at a doll hospital or a theatrical supply house. The easiest way to make this kind of wig is to first fit the doll's head with a cloth cap. Sew the hair onto this at the part, then spread paste or glue on the rest of the cloth cap and press the hair down onto this.

5 — Cut strips of fringe from felt, making the strands of the fringe not more than ¼ inch apart. Beginning at the forehead, glue or sew the fringe onto the doll's head, spacing each row to overlap the uncut edge of the previous row. This effect is particularly good on a modernistic doll, far more in keeping than natural hair would be.

Whatever kind of wig is used, be sure to fasten it in place securely, either by sewing invisibly at the hairline or by gluing it in place.

Patterns are included in this chapter for clothes for the dolls shown here, and may be copied exactly, or used as a guide for making other garments. In Chapter 9 we will go into detail about doll clothes, but now the most important thing to mention is that soft, fine materials are the best ones to use, rather than stiff, heavy ones. And don't forget to work carefully, without rushing through the various steps of making rag dolls.

3

Paper Dolls, Then, Now, and How

Perhaps you'll never own a rare, antique china doll dressed in real brocade and lace, but a paper doll — wearing a costume from any period of history — can be made as quickly as your fingers move. She can have a crown of gilt paper and a court dress fashioned of paper lace and filmy tissue, sprinkled with rosebuds cut from a gift card. Or the same figure can be turned into a modern fashion doll simply by changing her hair style, shoes, and dress. Illustrations in books, magazines, and newspapers will supply you with ideas.

The first paper dolls may have been made in China, long before the western world had even seen paper, because paper was probably invented by the Chinese. It wasn't brought to Europe until the twelfth century, but before long, paper making had become an important industry on the continent. Perhaps one of the first uses for paper was in the making of paper dolls.

There are no dolls surviving from those early days, but we do have a few animated paper dolls that were made in the seventeenth century. These jointed, movable dolls were called Jumping Jacks or, more often, Pantins, from the name of the French town where they originated. The amusing figures, manipulated by pulling a string threaded through the back, were first made only for children. But soon they became a craze with adults. Some of the most famous artists of the day designed Pantins, in sizes varying from four inches to two feet. Men and women of the French court collected Pantins, carried them about, made them dance, and tried to outdo each other in the size and value of their collections.

You can make Pantins for your collection, dressing them in the typical Jumping Jack costume, or as dancers, clowns, or acrobats. The illustrations in this chapter show how to cut and string them.

Paper dolls, as we commonly think of them, were first made and sold in Europe about 1791. One set was advertised as being the figures of young women, dressed in underclothes and a corset, and packed with sets of six complete costumes. The dolls were about 8 inches high and were packaged with the suggestion that they ". . . can be easily carried in a handbag or workbox to give amusement at parties or to children."

In the 1800's, pockets in the backs of children's books contained paper dolls illustrating the stories. About the same time, American manufacturers began to sell bound copies of sheets of paper dolls. At first they were printed in black and white, then tinted by hand. They were expensive, and it wasn't till 1880 that dolls could be printed cheaply enough so that every girl could have a family of paper dolls.

As happened with rag dolls, paper dolls of many kinds were designed and patented from 1800 through the 1900's. Again as with rag dolls, many paper dolls were given as premiums with such varied products as coffee, dyes, bicycles and spices.

Godey's Lady's Book featured paper dolls in 1859 and was one of the first magazines to do so. It was quickly followed by other magazines and many newspapers. Early in the 1900's, there was a great flood of magazine dolls, including those in *Delineator*, *Pictorial Review*, *Good Housekeeping*, and — in 1908 — the *Ladies' Home Journal*.

Perhaps the most famous of all magazine dolls were those in

Call him Pantin or Jumping Jack. He will dance and wave his arms
when you pull strings fastened to his back. Punch small holes only
through arm and leg pieces for strings. Knot threads, and run through
body piece, arms, and legs, knot again on other side, clip thread ends.

the beloved Lettie Lane series, designed by Sheila Young. They appeared month after month and were followed by the Betty Bonnet series in the same magazine, the *Ladies' Home Journal*. Doll collectors pay premium prices today for complete copies of the magazines carrying Lettie Lane or Betty Bonnet, for it is hard to find old *Journals* that have not had the paper-doll pages removed.

Rose O'Neill's "million-dollar baby," the Kewpie, which was made in the round in china, celluloid and stockinet, appeared for the first time as a paper doll in the *Woman's Home Companion*, in 1910. From month to month an entire magazine page was devoted to new adventures of enchanting Kewpies, with their fat, baby bodies and tiny blue wings.

It's impossible to list all the paper dolls of the past, for they were sold or given away almost everywhere. But we can thank the doll lovers who appreciated and saved the specimens that still exist, and we can profit by their wisdom.

Nowadays, dime, drug, and toy stores have many books of paper dolls. Some of these dolls are printed in color on glazed paper, others in black and white outline, ready to be colored at home. Wise collectors stay alert and buy interesting sets as soon as they appear. Most editions are limited, and once a printing is exhausted it's unlikely to be reprinted. These books, which cost only a few cents, will some day be even more valuable than the Lettie Lanes and Betty Bonnets, for they do a substantial job of recording modern history, dress, hair styles, accessories, personalities, movies and the theater.

As examples, there were many paper-doll books of the Dionne quintuplets in the 1930's, but you can't buy one now at the corner drug store. At the time of the coronation of Queen Elizabeth II, paper-doll books appeared with pictures of all the royal family, in their various costumes. During World War II, a book had paper dolls dressed as Waves, Wacs, and women Marines. Try to find one now!

We've been talking about paper dolls you buy. But, as is true with other kinds of dolls, your paper-doll collection will have more meaning if you make dolls yourself. The only materials required are scraps of cardboard, wrapping or letter paper, colored pencils or crayons, India ink, and a drawing pen. By adding gift-wrapping paper, lace-paper doilies, tissue and crepe paper, you can dress glamorous ladies and handsome gentlemen in the most elaborate costumes.

Best of all, a large family of paper dolls can live very compactly in a drawer, on a shelf, or between pages of a scrapbook. If you want to take them with you on a trip, just slip them into an envelope and tuck them into your suitcase. They won't take up much space, and you may be able to fit them out with hula skirts or parkas, drawn from life.

My own first paper dolls, drawn for me by a neighbor when I was four years old, were the most wonderful dolls I ever owned. The doll mother wore a yellow-satin ball gown, and her little daughter a white Sunday-school dress trimmed with lace and velvet ribbon, and a wide pink sash — all of paper.

Years later, I made paper dolls for my own daughters until they learned to make dolls for themselves. Sometimes they drew their own designs, and sometimes they cut figures from fashion magazines and mounted them on heavy cardboard. Then they would cut out pictures of tables, beds, chairs, and rugs and spread the furniture for each room arrangement out on the floor. For hours they would walk the dolls through the rooms, pretending the dolls were talking and changing costumes.

Incidentally, if you include pictures of room furnishings with your dolls, you'll have a valuable record of interior decoration, as well as of clothing styles.

Paper dolls are the quickest, easiest dolls in the world to make for yourself, and the illustrations here will give you a good idea of how to do it.

First, trace onto thin paper the outlines of the dolls shown here. Next, using a soft pencil on the wrong side of the paper, go over this outline. Then place the drawing, face up, on a piece of white Bristol board, and go over the outline with a sharp pencil. This will transfer the outline onto the Bristol board.

Draw the features with a pen and India ink. Then tint the hair, eyes, mouth and cheeks with colored pencils, crayons, or

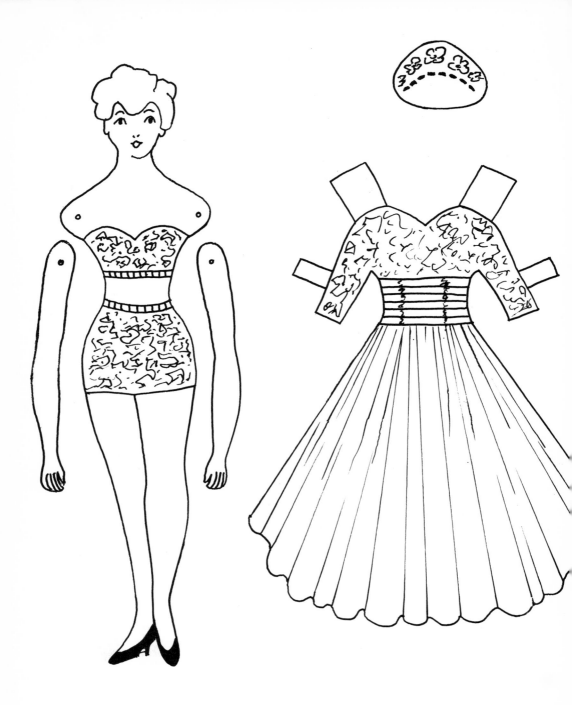

Basic pattern for woman or young girl can be changed slightly to make either modern or old-fashioned doll. One dress is shown, with a hat that can become a crown for a queen or a halo for a bride.

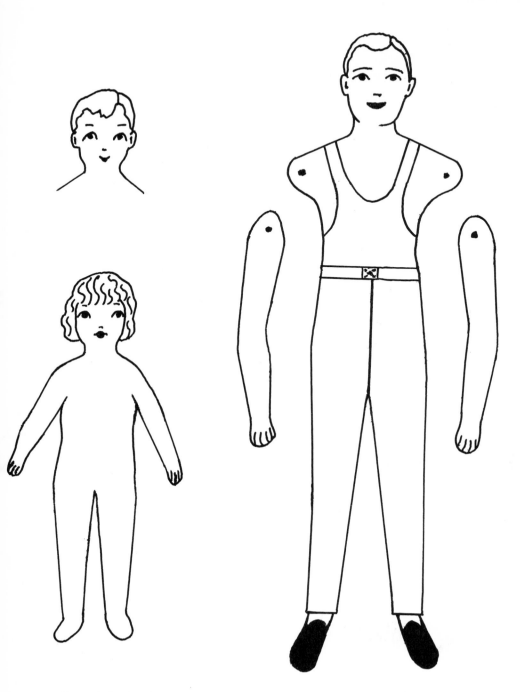

Man of the family is ready to put on a business suit or sports clothes. Substitute the boy's head for that of the girl on the child figure, and dress them as brother and sister.

watercolor. Do this smoothly and with a light touch; a delicate color is better than a crude, bold one.

Cut out the doll along the outside line. If you want it to stand up, turn up the legs at the ankles and paste the soles of the feet onto a strip of heavy cardboard. You can reinforce the doll by pasting another piece of cardboard to cover the back, or you can paste a piece of muslin over the doll's back.

If you want to make an even firmer base for holding the doll erect, consult the illustrations for three different kinds of stands.

Paper-doll clothes can be made of watercolor paper, typewriter paper, printed gift-wrap, wallpaper, tissue paper, crepe paper, details from old Valentines and Christmas cards, lace paper, strips of cotton lace, thin silk or muslin, ribbon, or almost any material than can be glued or pasted into place.

In making a doll dress, the first step is to draw lightly around the figure of the doll with pencil. Sketch in the details, and draw a tab at each shoulder and at the waistline to hold the costume in place. Color the dress or suit and cut it out carefully.

Hats are made with a slit, as shown in the drawing of the bride's veil, to hold them in place on the doll's head.

Another way to make paper-doll clothes is to cut them double. Leave the neck opening big enough to insert the head, or cut a slit on the back of the dress wide enough to insert the head. If you cut the garment double, you don't need shoulder tabs.

You can make an entire paper-doll family from the drawings shown here. Or, by varying hair styles and shoes, you can turn the dolls into people of different eras — from cave men to astronauts.

In 1870, the McLaughlin Bros. paper dolls were packaged in boxes 6 by 3 inches, and 2 inches deep, an idea you could use in storing your own dolls. The outside of the box was covered with paper which imitated brick, with steps leading up to a door. On either side of the door were long windows with lace curtains. A strip of picket fence divided the steps from the front walk. The size of the box suggests that the dolls it once held were 5 or 6 inches tall.

Left — Devices for holding dolls upright: 1) small block of wood cut through center, to hold feet; 2) glue ends of strip together; 3) cut slits on center lines and fit pieces together a right angles. Right — Man and girl this size suit small paper theater.

Another good way to keep your paper dolls is to make separate paper envelopes for each doll and its clothes. Decorate the outside of the envelope with cutout pictures and the doll's name. File the envelopes upright in a box. A large number of dolls may be stored this way in a small space.

One of the most fascinating paper-doll projects is the making and use of a paper theater, with paper dolls as the actors. Make paper furniture and scenery, or use dollhouse furniture. Even china and celluloid dolls can be used in the theater, dressed in costume.

Paper-doll actors will be more interesting if they are jointed at shoulders and knees. Then they can move their arms and walk or dance. But whether they're jointed or not, you must have some way to move them on and off stage. A simple way to do this is to modify the way marionettes are strung. Tie one end of a heavy black thread to the doll's head and the other end to a short stick. By tilting or moving the stick, you can make the doll walk or dance. If the doll's arms and legs are movable, tie a thread to each hand. With a little practice you can control the feet by raising and lowering the threads of the hands with a slight jerk.

You will learn to manipulate a doll in each hand. And if you call on a friend to help you, you can put as many as four dolls on the stage at one time. Or you can tie several dolls to a long stick and create the effect of a chorus line.

This paper theater could also be made of wood, and with minor changes the same diagrams could be used for building a puppet theater.

Get a heavy cardboard carton about 25 inches long and 16 inches wide. It should be at least 16 inches deep. Turn it bottom side up and cut off three sides so they'll be 4 inches deep, as shown in (a). Cut the fourth side 16 inches deep. Fold this wide side up as shown in (b) and (c) and glue it in position, with the extension 12 inches higher than the 4-inch sides. This part will be the actual stage and the extension will hold the scenery. That's why it's folded double — for extra strength.

Make scenery for the backdrop by cutting trees or mountains

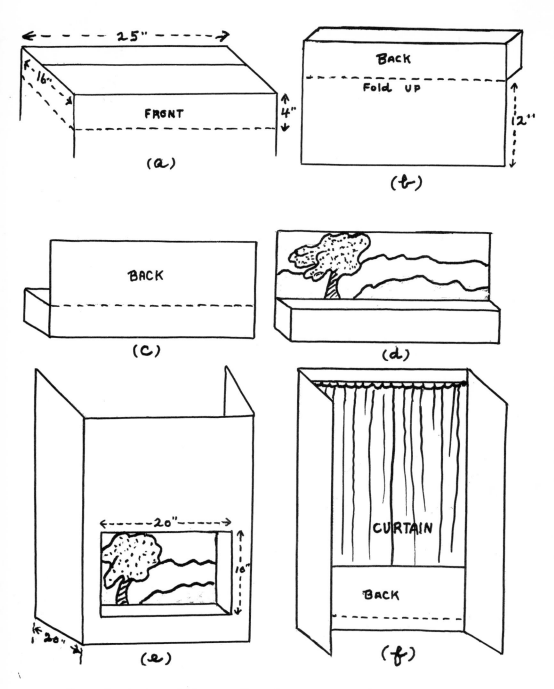

Paper theater is made from cardboard cartons. It may be set on table during performances, then folded for storage in a closet.

from colored paper and gluing them to the extension. You can make other scenes on cardboard cut the same size as the extension. When changing scenes, simply fasten the background you wish to the top of the extension with paper clips. See (d).

Take a larger cardboard carton and cut off three sides to make a screen, as in (e). The height of this screen depends on the height of the person who will operate the theater. It should be high enough to conceal the operator as she stands by the table and moves the actors. Instead of using a carton, you can make this screen of one large sheet of cardboard, folded.

Cut an oblong opening in the screen 4 inches from the lower edge, as in (e). Glue the front of the stage base to the bottom of the screen so they will be at table level. Leave the wings of the screen free.

Make a curtain of soft, opaque cloth and sew small curtain rings to the top. Fasten a heavy wire near the top of the screen and run the rings along it (f). This curtain can be operated easily by the person behind the scenes, without being seen by the audience.

Decorate the front of the theater with craft or gift paper.

This theater is manipulated from the top, just like a marionette theater. There's plenty of space above the backdrop to move the actors. If more than one person works behind scenes, spread the wings of the screen to conceal them from the audience.

Books in the library will supply many one-act plays suitable for paper-doll theaters, or you can write your own plays. If you have a helper, one of you can read the parts and the other move the dolls. Use a record player for musical effects, or go even farther and present an entire recording of a ballet or operetta, complete with voices and music. All you have to do is move the dolls at the proper times.

This theater could have endless variations as a school or club entertainment, as the highlight at a birthday party for small children, as a money-making project, or just for fun for yourself and your friends.

4

Meet the Wood Children

The dolls who lived in Racketty-Packetty house had once lived a gay, fashionable life. But Cynthia moved the house into a corner of the nursery — not the best corner, either — and neglected the dolls until they became shabby and tattered. She even changed their names from Charlotte, Amelia, Clotilda, and Charles Edward Stuart to Meg and Peg and Kilmanskeg and Peter Piper, while Leontine, who had once been the family beauty, was called Ridiklis. After all Leontine's paint was licked off by a Newfoundland puppy, someone painted onto her wooden face a bright red spot for each cheek, a turned-up nose, round saucer-blue eyes and a comical mouth.

Racketty-Packetty house had belonged to Cynthia's grandmother before the days when Victoria was queen. All the dolls were jointed Dutch dolls, made of wood, so it was easy to paint any kind of features on them and push their arms and legs into any position. The dolls went on for years, trying to make the best of their sad neglect, until Cynthia suddenly learned to appreciate them. As Peter Piper would cheerfully say, "Who cares! Let's join hands and have a dance."

New England wooden doll dressed in pantalets. Arms and legs are painted white to knees and elbows, fastened to body with small nails.

Two English dolls: 1700 wooden baby has arm legs fastened by method used for larger do bisque nurse is doll-house size — 6 inches.

Then the dolls would join hands and dance round and round, kicking up their heels until their rags and tatters flew about, and they'd laugh until they fell down, one on top of the other.

The story ends happily when "the little girl princess" carries them off to "a splendid palace."

Frances Hodgson Burnett told about the Racketty-Packetty house and the adventures of its Dutch dolls in a delightful story published in 1906. The illustrations by Harrison Cady show "their nice, queer faces and their funny clothes," with Ridiklis before and after she was turned into a beauty again, and got back her real name of Leontine.

The little girl princess could have been the little girl who later became the queen of England, for Victoria's collection of 132 Dutch dolls, which she and her governess dressed, are famous today and are in the Victoria and Albert Museum in London.

The doll family of Racketty-Packetty house shares honors with other famous Dutch dolls, in books and stories written by other authors. An entire series of stories by Florence and Bertha Upton was written about Dutch dolls. The first story, *The Adventure of Two Dutch Dolls and a Golliwog,* was followed by *Golliwog Tales,* all of them written many years ago.

48

Wooden dolls made in Germany after World War II are beautifully finished but dressed in shoddy cloth. Wooden feet give them solid base.

Another favorite story about a wooden doll is *Hitty, Her First Hundred Years,* by Rachel Field. Wooden dolls also appear in the stories of Kathleen Ainsley, which were published about the same time as the Upton stories. There seems to be something about wooden dolls that fires the imagination of storytellers, for there are other books about them, some popular for several generations.

Dutch dolls, also sometimes called Flanders Babies, Penny Woodens, and peggity dolls, range in size from those only half an inch high, to large ones of 20, 22, or even 24 inches. Although wooden dolls are seldom beautiful, their rosy cheeks and shiny painted hair are irresistible. They're made in sections, with head and body usually carved from a single piece of wood and the arms and legs fastened in place with small nails or pins in such a way that they can be moved.

The strangest thing about Dutch dolls is that most of them weren't Dutch at all, but German. The name Dutch Doll is probably a corruption of their earlier name "Deutsche Doll" — German Doll — for most of them came from families of woodcarvers who lived in the forests of Germany. The dolls were carved at home and brought to town to be traded to merchants for food and clothing. The merchants, in turn, sold them to other merchants, all over Europe. It's impossible to trace the origin of most old wooden dolls, for few of them are marked or dated.

The smallest doll in my own collection is a wooden baby less than one inch long, dressed in a long, lace-trimmed dress. Its tiny arms and legs are movable, and the features are painted with red and black paint. Dabs of black paint on the feet represent shoes. It is said to date back to the time of Queen Anne, about 1700, and came from a Canadian antique shop. The wooden baby is in the arms of a much more recent bisque doll nurse, in cap and uniform. The price of the pair was based entirely on the value of the wooden baby: 20 dollars for a toy that probably was first sold for only a penny.

Wooden dolls were made by the first New England colonists, but it wasn't until Joel Ellis invented and patented his wooden doll in 1873 that wooden dolls were made commercially. Ellis was a clever and determined Yankee who had a large toy factory in the little town of Springfield, Vermont. He had abundant wood and water power to work with, and although fires and floods wiped out his factory twice, he persisted in his business with all the spirit of a true American pioneer. His patented doll was made with double mortise-and-tenon joints that gave it friction enough to hold any position, and came in three sizes: small, 12 inches; medium, 15 inches; and large, 18 inches. There are many Joel Ellis dolls in existence today, even though he made them for only one year. His business ability apparently didn't equal his persistence and craftsmanship, for he was forced to close the factory and leave Springfield.

What happened next is another of the strange stories about dolls. In the small village of Springfield were many other toy-makers, and they adapted Ellis's patents, added new ones, combined and improved methods of manufacture and left us a jumbled combination of inventions that were sold under the town name. Springfield dolls owe their existence to Joel Ellis, F. D. Martin, George W. Sanders, Henry H. Mason, Luke W. Taylor, and C. C. Johnson. Springfield dolls seem to have been

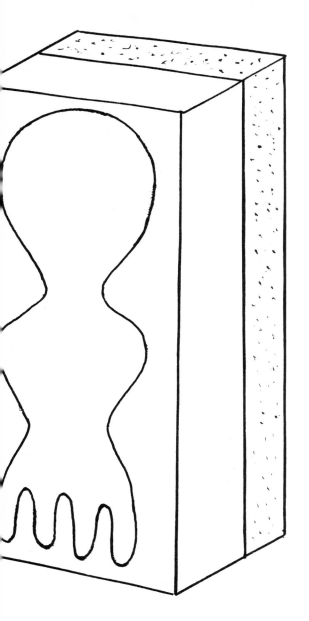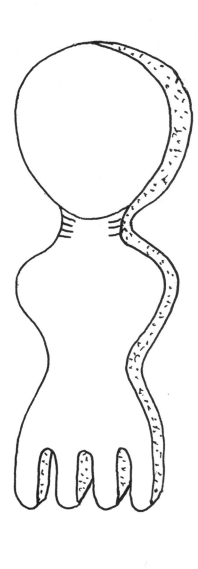

For head and body of wooden doll, use piece of soft wood 5 inches long, 2 inches wide, 1½ inches thick. Saw on solid lines. Head to neck is 1 inch wide. Taper doll at neck so body is ½ inch thick.

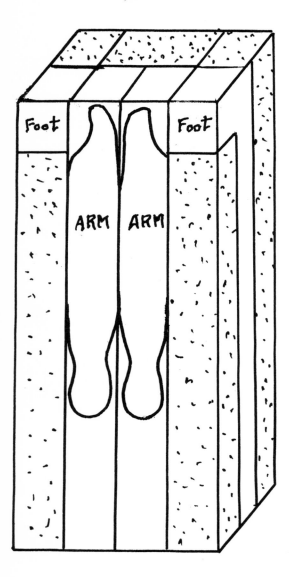

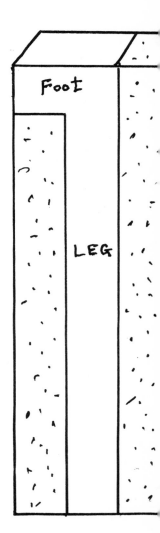

For arms and legs, saw another 5-inch piece of soft wood into sections as shown. Shape them with sharp knife. Shape leg tops to fit into slots of body section. Fasten arms and legs with small finishing nails.

made in the spirit of the New England town meeting, and have become a real American tradition.

The wooden dolls we've been talking about are all dolls of the past, but there are many wooden dolls being made today. As you travel over the world, you can find coffee-wood dolls in Ceylon, Balinese bamboo bell dolls, African dolls made of native wood, and wooden dolls in South America, Italy, the South Pacific, Holland, Germany, Mexico, and Japan. The Grenfell Mission in Labrador makes Eskimo dolls dressed in fur, leather and cloth, but only the heads are wood, because Labrador's supply of wood is scarce. They can still be classed as wooden dolls.

Soon after the end of World War II, I received a request from a young German who was anxious to exchange wooden dolls for food parcels, and pictures of some of those he sent me are shown in this chapter. The cheap, coarse cloth used to dress them is a reminder that Germany was then suffering from a shortage of most kinds of manufactured goods. These dolls, which came from a country that was once the heart of the toymaking industry, are pathetic, beautifully made and carefully painted. They add something sad to the long story of dolls.

In the previous chapter, I gave a pattern for making a paper Jumping Jack. You can use the same pattern and make one from thin plywood instead. Trace the pattern onto the wood and cut it out with a jig saw. Paint it in bright colors with tempera or oil paint, and give the doll a final coat of shellac. String it just as you would the paper doll, but use heavier cord.

You might change the pattern slightly to make Santa Claus figures, painting the clothes bright red, trimmed with white. Paint the shoes black.

Making dolls like this would be a good club or craft project, and you might sell them at Christmas time. Don't forget to keep one for your own doll collection.

With a piece of wood, a jig saw, and a sharp jackknife, you can next make a Dutch doll. Take a piece of soft pine or balsa wood. The balsa is easier to carve, but the pine is better, because it won't splinter as easily and will hold the pins or nails for the joints more firmly.

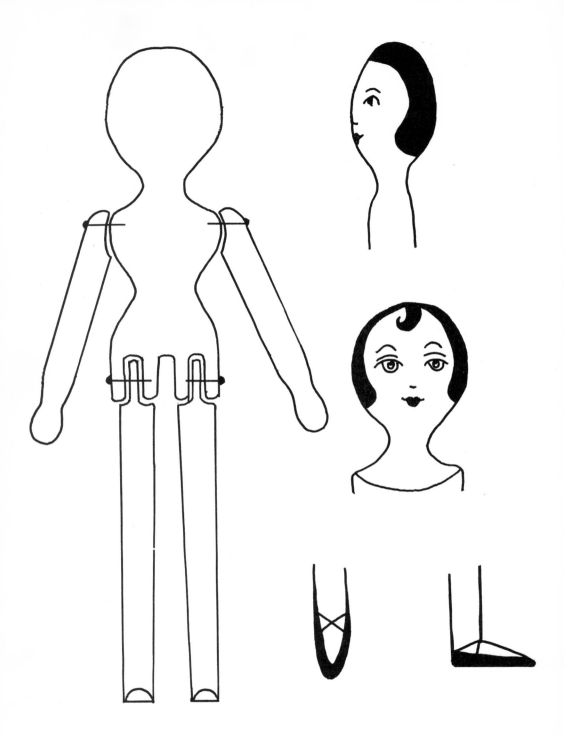

Doll assembled, ready to paint. Details of painting on head and feet.

Follow the instructions for making the doll, and when it's completed, sandpaper each piece carefully before you assemble the parts. Paint it as shown in the picture, using white-enamel paint, and let the paint dry. Add extra coats the same way until the grain of the wood is well covered. Add the features with a small brush dipped in oil paint which has been tinted with red for the lips and cheeks, and blue for the eyes. To be truly authentic, the doll should have black hair. Dress her in clothes made of any fine, soft cloth, preferably in pantalets and an 1850-style dress.

Someday an author will write a story about a wooden peddler doll. Doll collectors have been enjoying them for many, many years, and there are never two exactly alike. Dress your wooden doll in the historical peddler black dress, long red cape, white apron, and black-silk bonnet over a white mob cap. Suspend a small, flat tray or basket on a waist-long cord around her neck and let it hang in front of her. Into the tray, put a stock of miniature sewing materials, books, spoons, knives, dishes, pans, and trinkets that come in gum and candy machines, tiny party favors, bits of costume jewelry, and almost any object too small to be displayed any other way. A peddler doll should be 12 or 15 inches high, rather than a smaller size.

I've mentioned only a few ways to make or dress a wooden doll. You'll probably think of many others. Whatever costume you choose, give your wooden doll an old-fashioned name: Ridiklis or Leontine, Peggity or Victoria, Sarah or Mehitabel; and give her an honored place with your family of dolls. Her ancestors were humble but enduring.

5

Heads of Paste and Paper

What is papier mâché? The French words mean chewed paper, but the paper is really torn or chopped, rather than chewed. Later in this chapter you'll learn how to make and use it.

Papier mâché was probably invented in China, thousands of years ago. Trade between Asia and Europe was slow and round-about, with no airplanes, trains or trucks to hurry goods from one continent to the other, and there were no magazines, newspapers, radios, or TV to report the news of discoveries and inventions. So it may have been several hundred years after the invention of papier mâché before it was even seen in Europe.

The first use of papier mâché in Europe was probably in the making of snuff boxes in Germany in 1740, although some historians claim that papier-mâché dolls had been made there 50 years before that. Once again we're reminded that dolls have been important for a great many years.

From almost the beginning of modern history, Germany was the toymaking center of Europe, and it continued to be until World War I. Most of the dolls and toys made there weren't the products of production-line factories, but of family and village projects. They were bought by wholesalers and sent all over the world.

Papier-mâché dolls and doll heads weren't made in America until 1858 but were all imported from Germany. Many of these dolls had set-in glass eyes and were beautiful. But they were not dated or labeled, so it's impossible to identify them.

The first patent ever issued by the U.S. Patent Office for any kind of doll was given to Ludwig Greiner of Philadelphia on March 30, 1858 for his papier-mâché doll heads. Greiner was probably a German immigrant whose family had been toymakers for generations. He used some of the methods and copied some of the styles of German dolls, adding improvements of his own. Other manufacturers learned a great deal from his work, just as you may do, for his application for the patent gave the exact process he used in making papier-mâché doll heads. This is what it says:

> The manner of preparation is as follows: one pound of white paper, when cooked, is beat fine, and then the water is pressed out, so as to leave it moist. To this is added one pound of dry Spanish whiting, one pound of rye flour, and one ounce of glue. This is worked until it is well mixed. Then it is rolled out with a roller to the required thickness. After it is cut into pieces required for the mold, it is molded. Wherever there is a part projecting out — for instance the nose — it must be filled with linen or muslin. This linen or muslin must be well saturated with a paste which consists of rye flour, Spanish whiting and glue. After the heads are molded, each head consisting of two parts, they are allowed to get about half dry. Then they are put into the mold again and the parts well saturated with the paste. At the same time linen or muslin is cut up into pieces to match the parts, and is also saturated with this paste and pressed on the inside of the parts. Then they are left to dry again as before. Then these parts are put together with the same composition as the head is made from. After this, when they are perfectly

Greiner-type papier-mâché head painted flesh color with black hair, brown eyes. Head is 5 inches from crown to bottom of shoulders.

Composition doll with real hair and set-in gla[s] eyes. A typical German doll, it was probab[ly] made before 1890, for it is not marked.

dry, a strip of the linen or muslin saturated with paste is laid inside of the head where the parts were put together, and a piece is also put over each shoulder and extending over the breast outside. Then they are painted with oil paint.

Greiner renewed the patent in 1872, so he must have made his doll heads for at least 20 years. Because they were sturdy and durable, there are a great many of these dolls still in existence. Prices keep rising higher and higher, for to a serious doll collector, a Greiner doll is an aristocrat of the doll world.

Greiner made only doll heads, but any doll with a Greiner head is called a Greiner doll. The heads vary in size from 2 to 12 inches in height; there are both blondes and brunettes; some have blue eyes, others brown. The only positive way to identify a Greiner doll is by the black-and-gold label bearing his name, which was put under the finish on the back of the shoulders near the center of the lower edge. Even if the label is missing, it is sometimes possible to see the place where it was once pasted.

The weak spot in most Greiner dolls is the cloth-filled tip of the nose, which is almost always badly worn, and sometimes entirely missing.

There is a strong family resemblance among all Greiner doll heads, but none at all among the bodies of the dolls. These were always made at home, and never in factories. Generally the bodies were made of cloth stuffed with sawdust and had leather or wooden arms and hands. Even this procedure varies, and sometimes the entire body was made of leather. Quite often a Greiner doll's body proportions are a little odd, with a body either too short or too tall for the head. This can always happen when a dollmaker works without any rules to guide her.

For several years after Greiner's first patent, other manufacturers took out patents for papier-mâché dolls that were a little different from his, either in methods or materials. Then in 1877, Lazarus Reichmann of New York City invented a composition of sawdust and glue, without paper. This material was easier to use than Greiner's papier mâché, and as soon as manufacturers discovered it, they stopped using paper pulp.

Reichmann's composition was one of the best materials ever invented for making dolls, and it put an end to papier-mâché doll manufacturing. Today, composition is still being improved, with resins and other ingredients added to make it stronger and more lifelike, until almost all modern dolls are being made of either composition or plastic, and very little else.

The stores are full of good composition dolls, worthy of any doll collection. You can also find used ones in thrift shops, which need only small touch-ups and a bath to restore them. The Patsy dolls made in the 1920's and the Shirley Temple dolls of the 1930's, as well as dozens of other makes, are well worth looking for, and their prices are moderate. A composition doll is as nearly time-proof as a doll can be, for even a good plastic doll, natural-looking though it may be, is hard, or impossible to repair.

When it comes to dolls of papier mâché, just about the only way to get one for your collection is to make it yourself, unless you're lucky enough to inherit one or wealthy enough to buy an old papier-mâché doll.

It's only fair to say that this is no project for a first try at doll-making. It takes patience and close attention to detail to make

Shirley Temple doll in original clothes. Made about 1930, this doll is fine quality composition. Among most popular dolls of all time.

Professional marionette has papier-mâché head hands. Hair's gray yarn, feet wood weighted b lead strips. Papier-mâché's lightness is idea

a papier-mâché head you can be proud of, and it's better to make one of the easier kinds of dolls first, before you attempt a Greiner-type head. Practice using papier mâché by making a puppet or marionette, which doesn't need to have the fine details of a doll head.

In the preceding three chapters, you have read about dolls of cloth, paper, and wood. A papier-mâché doll combines all three materials, having a head of paper and a cloth body stuffed with sawdust.

When you made papier-mâché puppets at school or camp, you probably first shaped a clay head, then covered it with bits of paper mixed with paste. As soon as the papier mâché was dry, you removed the clay and finished the papier mâché with tempera paint. This method would be all right to use for making a very large doll head, but if you want the features to be clearly molded on a small doll head it's better to press the paper pulp *into* a mold.

Trace the illustration of the doll head shown here, and use it to guide you in modeling a head from clay. Be careful to locate the features as they are shown and to make the nose and chin clear-cut. You won't be able to get fine detail in the papier

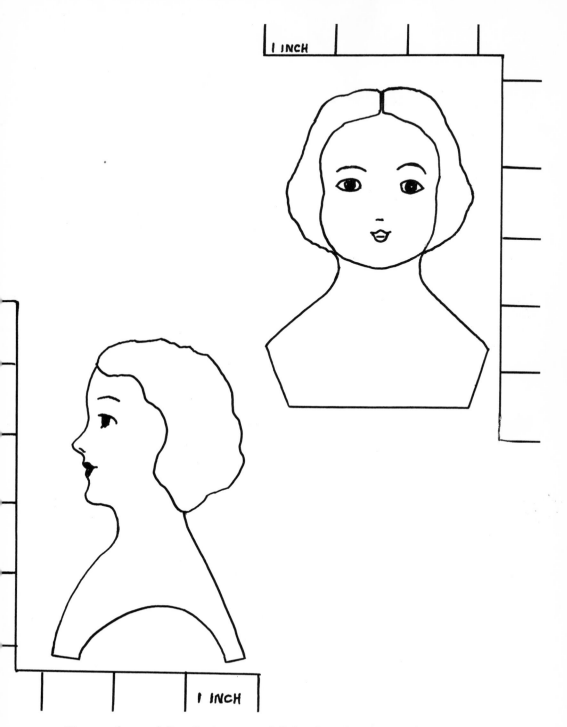

Diagram for modeling Greiner-type doll head, to be cast in plaster.

mâché, so work most of all for the bolder planes and angles of the face. Be sure there are no undercuts, that is, places where the clay turns under, as might happen under the chin. These act as hooks to hold the clay in the mold. Think of the way a hard-cooked egg slips out of the shell when it is cut exactly in half, or the way gelatine slides out of a mold after it has hardened. This is the way the head will have to slip out of the mold.

When the modeling is finished, dip your fingers into water, and smooth the clay head carefully. Then cut down through the head with a fine wire, making the parting line come from the top of the head through the highest part of the shoulders. You'll now have the front of the head in one piece and the back of the head in another.

Take two cardboard boxes about 2 inches wider and longer than the head pieces, and grease or oil them thoroughly all over the inside. Place each head section flat side down in a separate box, and press it down firmly.

Pour about 2 cups of water into a mixing bowl and into it sift plaster of Paris until a little island of plaster stands above the water. Mix with a spoon, stirring under the surface to avoid making air bubbles in the mixture. Stir every few minutes. In 15 or 20 minutes the plaster will begin to thicken. As soon as it will hold a faint mark when you draw your finger across the top of the plaster, work quickly and dip the plaster over the clay until the head is covered with about 2 inches of plaster. Jiggle the box slightly, to level the top surface, then allow to stand undisturbed while the plaster sets. When it is hard, peel off the cardboard box and remove the clay from the mold. Trim the top edges of the mold and put it aside for several days to dry thoroughly. This same mold can be used over and over again, so handle it gently.

While the molds are drying, get the materials ready for making the papier-mâché head. Make a jar of paste by slowly mixing 1 cup of water with 2 tablespoons of flour until there are no lumps. Put this in a pan over low heat and bring it to a boil, then pour it into a covered jar to cool.

Plaster of Paris mold with papier-mâché head just as it comes from mold, before trimming and filling joint between two sections.

Buy a package of powdered papier mâché at a craft or hobby shop. This material is sold under different trade names, but the basic ingredient is papier mâché. It will make a smoother doll head than paper that you shred at home. Soak about 2 cups of this powder in water overnight.

Grease the inside of the dried plaster molds with Vaseline, cold cream, or cooking fat, taking care to see that the tip of the nose is also well greased but not filled with the fat. Rub grease over the flat top of the mold.

Put the softened papier mâché into a sieve, and press out as much water as possible. Then place the damp papier mâché in a bowl and add enough of the paste to make a stiff dough. Mix and knead it until papier mâché and paste are thoroughly combined.

Now line the plaster molds with the dough, pressing it down firmly. Be sure to push it down well into the nose, chin, and eye depressions. Pack the dough smooth with the back of a spoon until the dough is about ¼ inch thick. This lining will shrink as it dries, so don't make the lining too thin. Level the dough at the edge of the mold and smooth it. Take the tip of a knife, and gently separate the extreme top edge of the dough slightly from the mold. Place the molds in a warm, dry place until the papier mâché gets thoroughly hard. This may take several days. When

63

completely dry, the papier mâché should come out of the mold with little urging.

Trim off all uneven places on the edges and apply a little white glue to them. Then fit the two halves together and hold them in place with rubber bands slipped over the head. Let the head dry overnight. Trim the joint with a razor blade and then glue strips of paper across the seam inside the shoulders to reinforce it. Trim off all uneven places on the rest of the head and fill low spots with a paste made by adding white glue to some of the dry papier-mâché powder. Pat this in place instead of rubbing it. When these patches are almost dry rub them firmly to make them smooth. Dry the head again and sandpaper it lightly.

Tear (don't cut) paper towels into strips about ½ inch wide. Soak the strips in water for a few minutes, and then press out the excess water. Brush the entire head with a smooth coating of the paste you made, then cover it with the toweling strips. Do not overlap the strips, but just allow them to meet, so that they will merge together smoothly. This is very important, because if you overlap the strips, the head will be covered with ridges, instead of being smooth.

Lay the first covering with the strips placed horizontally. Apply a second covering of paste. Cover the head with a second layer of strips, this time placing them vertically, at right angles to the first layer. Two layers of strips should be enough to cover the head smoothly. But if you add other layers, alternate the direction in which you place them.

Take a modeling tool or your fingers and smooth the head firmly around the eyes, nose and mouth. Let the head dry, and then brush on a coat of shellac or clear lacquer. When this is dry, you'll be ready to paint the head.

For painting, use white enamel and tint it flesh color with a dab of red oil paint and a smaller dab of yellow. Add the oil color slowly and mix well. It should be a delicate flesh color, neither pinkish nor yellowish. Paint the entire head with this flesh color, and allow it to get perfectly dry. Then apply a second coat. Add more coats if necessary until you have a smooth surface, drying between each application.

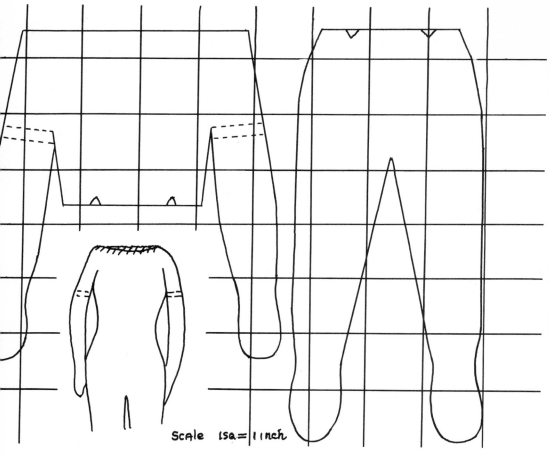

Scale 1sa = 1 inch

Body pattern for Greiner-type head. Trace pattern on paper, matching at notches. Cut 2 pieces, allowing ⅛-inch seam on all sides. Stitch together on pencil line.

Using the illustration as a guide, draw the features lightly on the head with a pencil. Tint one spoonful of white enamel with blue or brown oil paint for the eyes and another with red paint for the mouth. The face will be prettier if you use soft colors rather than vivid ones. Paint the features with the smallest-size watercolor brush. Don't try to make eyelashes; they cheapen the looks of the doll. Rub a tiny bit of pink enamel onto the doll's cheeks with your finger, as if you were applying rouge. Blend the edges carefully. Let the paint dry for several days.

Use the pattern shown here to make a cloth body for the doll. Fine white muslin or percale is good material. Stuff the body with sawdust. It's always easy to get as much sawdust as you want at a cabinet shop or lumberyard, where it's thrown away. Sift the sawdust through a colander or coarse sieve to remove bits of wood that would make the doll body lumpy.

Stuff the cloth body firmly, pressing the sawdust down with your fingers or the handle of a wooden spoon. Fill the body almost to the top, then use overcast stitches to sew together the edges of the opening.

Brush white glue inside the shoulders of the doll head and push them down snugly onto the stuffed body. Bind the head and body together with strips of cloth until the glue hardens.

Your doll will be almost unbreakable and will make an interesting addition to a well-rounded doll collection. Paint your name and the date in tiny letters on the back of her shoulders, so that a hundred years from now, experts will know that you, not Ludwig Greiner, made her.

6

Turn Candles Into Dolls

Dorothea is as beautiful as Cinderella at the ball, her creamy complexion flushed with petal pink. She has shining, violet-blue eyes, and her long yellow curls are fastened high on her head with a tiny ivory comb. When you hold her in your arms, her eyelids close, and the blond lashes brush against her cheeks.

She wears a trailing wine-colored dress trimmed with rhinestones, and the turquoise rings in her pierced ears match the color of the bows on her flat-heeled slippers.

Dorothea's skin looks so real that you're surprised when you touch it and discover it's wax. Her slender arms and hands and her slim legs have the same satiny feeling, but her body is made of white leather. Dorothea is a wax doll, and from the curve of her forehead to the tips of her sand-colored shoes, she's lovely.

Wax? Who ever heard of a doll made of wax? By now you must be used to hearing that for thousands of years dolls have been made from many different kinds of materials. Examine Dorothea closely, for her family history is older than Christianity. Dorothea's first ancestors were natives of Egypt, Greece and Rome thousands of years ago, when idols used in religious cere-

Top — Waxed face mask to be glued onto rag doll. Left — Old wax-doll head. Right — A 40-year-old wax doll with sawdust-filled cloth body.

monials were made of solid wax. This does *not* mean that the word doll is an abbreviation of the word idol, as you may have suspected. Instead, doll means Dorothea or Dorothy. Why? Who in the world was the first Dorothy? No one knows, but just for fun we gave that name to our wax Dorothea.

During the Middle Ages, Europeans made wax figures as votive offerings, and they made candle dolls in the form of saints and angels, in sizes ranging from less than an inch high to life-sized. Beeswax was easy to mold and color; in spite of some of its faults, it became more and more popular all over Europe. It wasn't strange that when dolls began to be made commercially, wax was one of the first materials used.

The earliest wax dolls were cast solid. But it was soon discovered that if papier mâché or composition were coated with wax, the dolls would be more durable and less likely to crack or melt.

While the center of the dollmaking industry was in Germany, for some reason England produced more wax dolls than any other country. It was in London that Dorothea was made about 1850, in the studio of Madame Augusta Montanari. This artist was head of the family that made the finest wax dolls in Europe, famous for inventing the method of laboriously inserting individual hairs in the wax with a hot needle to make wigs, eyelashes, and eyebrows. The Montanaris were not the only English artists to plant hair this way, but because few wax dolls were marked with the name of the maker, it is hard to identify them.

Many doll collectors have never seen a genuine Montanari doll except in museums, for the dolls were expensive and wax is perishable. However, no doll story is complete without mentioning them.

Beautifully modeled Dorothea is made of poured wax. Wax dolls of the following generation had heads that were poured into molds to form a shell of wax; still later, metal, papier-mâché and finally composition heads were used as the base for waxing. These are called *waxed* dolls, instead of *wax* and, of course, were much more lasting than the all-wax type. Most of the wax dolls we see today are of the waxed kind.

Most wax dolls have beautifully made glass eyes set into their heads, and these eyes were always made in Germany. The eyes were blue, brown, or the purplish shade of blue like that in Dorothea's. Eyes such as these were also used in china dolls and in some of papier mâché. There's nothing being made today that can compare with them.

Old wax dolls usually had heads only of wax, with bodies of cloth or leather. Sometimes the hands and legs were wax, but more often they were of the same material as the body.

It's hard to identify American-made wax dolls, because few of them are marked. None are being made today commercially. A few are imported, chiefly from Mexico and South America. Kimport Dolls recently mentioned a pair of modern dolls 5½ inches high with bodies of solid wax, from Mexico. The dolls wore clothes that had been waxed after they were dressed and they carried different kinds of burdens; fagots, red-clay jars, baskets, fruit. fish, or vegetables. Never pass up a chance to buy such dolls. Wax is hard to find, but not expensive, and wax dolls are charming.

While you may never find an old wax doll in perfect condition, it is not hard to restore one that needs only rewaxing.

After you've made a wax doll for yourself, you'll be able to renew an old head with little difficulty.

So, since every doll collection should have a wax doll — and because old ones are hard to find — the answer is to make one for yourself. With wax candles as an inexpensive and plentiful source of material, the kind of wax used for dolls is no longer limited to pure beeswax. You have a much better and more lasting material at hand than Madame Montanari ever dreamed of if you use non-drip wax candles or the squatty little votive candles, for sale even in supermarkets and dime stores. Do *not* use paraffin candles.

First make a papier-mâché head, as described in the previous chapter. If you want to make waxed arms and legs to use with it, model an arm and leg of clay, following the illustrations here, and make two-piece molds of plaster just as you made the mold for the head. Fill the molds with papier mâché, just as you made the head. When the papier-mâché parts are waxed, make a cloth body, again following the drawings and pictures and attach arms, legs and head as shown.

Now let's go back to examine the method of waxing: you should first enamel the papier mâché, painting the features. Let the enamel dry thoroughly.

Use a large juice can or some other container deeper than the height of the head and place the can in a pan of water to be heated on the stove. Put white candles in the can and add a small piece of red candle and a smaller piece of yellow candle or Crayola, to make a pale flesh color. Melted wax will be a different shade after it hardens, so test the color by dipping a strip of white cardboard into the melted wax. Never go away and leave wax heating on the stove, for wax is highly flammable.

When the wax has melted and you've tested the color and found it right, turn off the heat and let the wax cool until it's almost ready to form a thin film on top. Meantime, stuff the doll head with paper so the wax will not run down inside the head. Quickly dip the entire head in the wax, covering it with one twist of your hand. Let the wax drain off for a moment, and then place the head in an upright position to harden. If you want a thicker coating of wax, dip the head once more. For the best effect, however, one dipping is better than two. With two, the features don't show through clearly.

If you let the head stay in the hot wax too long, some of the enamel may slide off. If it does, dip the head in warm water to remove all the wax, and start from the beginning. You'll have to let the head dry before repainting, and dry again after painting, before you wax it. It's a good idea to practice dipping something of similar size before you attempt the painted head.

After the wax is completely hard, rub it with a soft cloth to give it a softly glossy finish.

Wax the arms and legs the same way. Then assemble the doll as described.

If you want to make a small, solid-wax doll, model a small one of clay and make a two-piece mold as you did before. Fill each half of the mold with melted wax and let it harden, then warm it slightly by dipping into hot water for a minute. Stick the tip of an icepick into the flat top of the wax to lift the halves out of the molds, then fasten the two sections together with a thin coating of melted wax. Heat a modeling tool and slide it carefully over the place where the two sections meet to cover the joint. Be careful not to mar any of the details of the figure when you do this.

This solid figure could be in the shape of a doll, a character for a Christmas nativity scene, or even a doll candle — if you insert a short length of candlewicking in the wax before you join the sections.

Candlemakers now produce a great variety of little colored-wax figures that you can call either dolls or candles. Just as with paper dolls, they are so plentiful and inexpensive that collectors sometimes overlook them. Some day they'll be antiques. A far-sighted collector will add a few of the best to her collection. Look for quality rather than quantity, and then take care of them by wrapping them in tissue paper. Even modern wax will fade and grow brittle if it's exposed too long to the light. Keep these figures in a moderate temperature, where heat won't melt, nor cold crack the wax.

7

What Is This One?

This chapter is a picture gallery of some of the china dolls in my own collection, with descriptions and comments about them. You'll notice that each doll has a name. Why not! Would *you* like to be known only as "that girl with brown eyes"?

China dolls were made for more than a hundred years before their top place was taken by dolls of composition and plastic. In one chapter, or even one book, it's impossible to mention them all. In the back of this book you'll find a list of other books that describe and give the manufacturers' marks of many more old dolls, to help you in identifying those you find. In addition, Janet Pagter Johl's book, *Your Dolls and Mine,* is a splendid guide to dolls made during the first half of this century, many of them not mentioned in any other doll book.

There are a few basic facts about china dolls to consider before we look at the pictures.

China is the name for objects made of clay and baked in a kiln. A kiln is a kind of oven that can be heated to a much higher temperature than the kitchen oven. In fact, a kiln must be hot enough to melt glass. This heating is called *firing*. After china has been fired, it's called *bisque*. It may then be covered with a form of liquid glass, called *glaze,* and fired again to give it a shiny surface.

Doll collectors have given special names and meaning to both bisque and glazed china. To them, a china doll always means one that's glazed, and is generally a bluish-white color. Some rare china dolls are a creamy white. If transparent glaze is used over pink clay, collectors call it pink luster, although this is not a true luster according to a potter's meaning of the word.

When doll collectors speak of French or German bisque, they mean unglazed pink or flesh-colored china. *Parian* is their name for unglazed white china, which looks almost like marble; stone or sugar bisque is a coarser grade of unglazed white china. As a rule, their top rating for glazed china goes to pink luster, and their top rating for unglazed china goes to Parian, although some of the European bisques are just as fine.

Until 1914, almost all china and bisque doll heads were made in Germany, even for the so-called French dolls. The earliest china doll heads were sold separately, to be attached to home-made bodies. A little later, complete dolls with china or bisque heads and papier-mâché or composition bodies were made in Germany and sometimes assembled there, where labor costs were low. Others were sent to France to be finished, and often labeled with French names. It's often hard to tell just where a certain doll did originate, for the marks are not standard.

In 1890, Congress passed a law requiring that all dolls imported into the United States be marked with the name of the country in which they were made. This helps us a little. Since very few dolls were made in any country outside of Europe, an old, un-marked china doll was probably either French or German.

One way to guess the age of a china doll is by its hair style. Early dolls have high, uncovered foreheads; later ones often wear bangs or clusters of curls down to their eyebrows.

Old dolls can also be dated by their shoes. If a doll wears flat shoes, it was probably made before 1860. After that, almost all dolls were made with high-heeled shoes.

73

Mother Parlington has a head of pink luster, was made in 1853. The author discovered Mother Parlington in an antique shop.

It was an old china doll that started me on my own doll collection during World War II. Our homesick daughter, Barbara, was to spend her first Christmas a continent away from her family, and an old china doll was something she had always wanted. The budget wouldn't stretch far enough for us to buy her a genuine old-fashioned doll, so I made one in my kitchen and had someone else fire, glaze, and paint her.

Abiatha Ann was far from perfect, but she looked very much like the 1885 doll named Agnes, shown in this chapter. She sat out the war in Oak Ridge, Tennessee, while Barbara worked there in the first atom factory. Before the war ended, I'd made and collected other china dolls, much better ones, but none as important as Abiatha Ann. Now it's time to open the gallery door and look at the pictures of some of them.

Mother Parlington's sweet face touched my heart the first time I saw her in a California antique shop. Her head is made of pink luster, and she has a high forehead, with hair smoothed back off her face — sure signs of an old doll. Her shiny black hair lies in flat curls at the back of her head. Her cloth body and white leath-

74

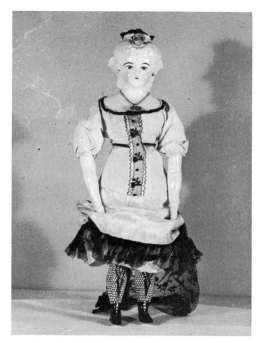

nes is a big girl of white glazed china, made
Germany. Her brown curls coiling over one
oulder and her pierced ears are unusual.

Violetta has silk skirts, black lace stockings.
She's white glazed china, nearly like many Parian dolls. Likely made around 1875 to 1880.

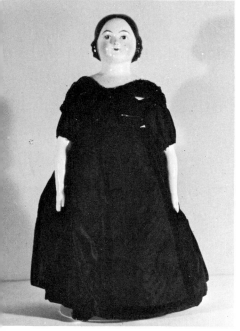

rnelia is probably about same age as Mother
lington, but almost twice as tall. Made —
bably in Germany — of white glazed china.

Mrs. Taunton's among last of unmarked German
china dolls. Hair-do dates her about 1890.
Muggity Ann: one of author's first china dolls.

er hands were homemade, before the days of sewing machines. She wears a black silk dress, white net cap and fichu. In her hands she holds a tiny wool sock which she is knitting on two straight pins. A brocaded knitting bag swings from her arm, and she looks at us through little wire-framed spectacles. She's only 9 inches tall. On her petticoat is pinned a yellowed slip of paper, and on it, in old-fashioned script, is written:

I am Mother Parlington. I came to visit Lillie Howell in 1853, and she persisted in my staying ever since.

Every time I visited the city where she lived, I went in to see her, just because she was so lovely. And although she wasn't for sale, her owner always took her out of the glass case and let me hold her. The last time I went in to say hello, her owner's eyes filled with tears when I went to the case.

"You love her, don't you?" she asked. Then she told me about her little granddaughter and the doll collection that was being made for her, with Mother Parlington as the oldest and best doll . . . then an accident that ended it all.

"Do you want the doll?" the woman asked. "You're the only one I'd let her go to — now."

Did I? Do you wonder that Mother Parlington means a great deal to me?

Mrs. Jonathan Briggs undoubtedly raised her children in way of all good ladies of 1885. She has red taffeta skirt and bustle at back.

8

Other Dolls

Fair Charlotte lived on a mountain side,
In a wild and lonely spot,
No dwelling was for three miles round
Except her father's cot.

On New Year's Eve when the sun was set,
She gazed with a wistful eye
Out of the frosty window forth,
To see the sleighs go by.

Then she weeps because she wants to go to the dance in the village, 15 miles away, but no one has asked her. Suddenly young Charlie's sleigh appears, and he dashes to the door and begs her to go with him. Her mother consents, but insists that she must wear a blanket to keep her warm. Fair Charlotte is stubborn and runs out of the house wrapped only in her silken cloak.

The night is bitterly cold, the snow is deep, Charlotte shivers, cries out, then seems to feel warm and goes to sleep.

When they reach the inn and the ride ends, Charles jumps from

77

the sleigh and holds out his hand to help Charlotte step out, but she doesn't move.

> *He asked her once, he asked her twice,*
> *She answered not a word;*
> *He asked her for her hand again,*
> *But still she never stirred.*
>
> *He tore her mantle from her brow,*
> *On her face the cold stars shone.*
>
> *Then swiftly through the lighted room*
> *Her lifeless form he bore.*
> *Fair Charlotte was a stiffened corpse*
> *And word spoke never more.*

One version of the ballad ends with this solemn warning:

> *Now, ladies, when you hear of this*
> *Think of that dreadful sight,*
> *And never venture thinly clad,*
> *On such a winter's night.*

There are 14 or 15 other verses of this New England ballad, which Phillips Barry once contributed to the *Journal of American Folklore*. He credited William Lorenzo Carter with the original ballad, based on a tragedy that once really happened in the mountains of Vermont. He calls Carter, born near Rutland, Vermont, in 1833, "a modern representative of the old-time wandering minstrel." The singer, born blind, roamed through the New England and Atlantic states, then went West, probably the reason this ballad has been found from Maine to the Dakotas, Oklahoma, and even in Nova Scotia. It was many years before the words were written down, so it's no wonder there are so many versions of it.

In addition to being a bit of real American folklore, the story of Fair Charlotte is one more instance of the meeting of dolls and history. For about the time that Carter began to travel around the country singing the ballad, Germany was sending us quan-

Antique and modern Frozen Charlottes. Upper left — Unglazed stone bisque. Upper right — Glazed china with black hair, 1¾ in. tall. Lower left — 2-in. unglazed china, from Japan. Lower right — 1-in. metal, unpainted.

tities of tiny, stiff dolls that were promptly given the name Frozen Charlottes.

They were also called penny dolls, for they cost one penny each. Another name for them was pillar dolls, because the arms and legs were made tight against the body. Some people called them cake dolls. When I was a little girl, my mother often took dolls just like the little black-haired doll in the picture and wrapped them in waxed paper for baking inside my birthday cake, for good luck.

Wedding-cake dolls were baked in a wedding cake, along with a ring, a penny and a thimble. Teacup dolls were used to stir the sugar in a cup of tea. Both of them were nothing in the world but Frozen Charlottes.

These little dolls vary in size from less than one inch to as tall as 15 inches, and materials include white, pink, or black glazed china; stone bisque and Parian; metal and wax. Some of the bodies are solid; others are hollow. Hair styles differ, as in the four dolls shown here. In fact, it's rare to find two Charlottes just alike. Perhaps this is because they have been made for so many years — from 1840, or even earlier, up to today. The tiny metal doll in the picture came from a modern-day gum machine.

Frozen Charlottes are ideal dolls to collect because even the old ones aren't expensive, and because they can be displayed in a small space. One collector keeps hers in a clear-glass vase, so they can be seen through the glass. Another keeps hers in an antique china shoe near a larger doll dressed as the Old Woman Who Lived in a Shoe.

You're likely to find what collectors call half dolls, most of which are neither rare nor valuable but worth adding to your collection. Some of the finest of these were made long ago in Germany and are not marked. Many of the figures have arms extended or upraised and look like Dresden figures. Perhaps some of them were made in Dresden molds. The china ends at the waistline, or just below, and there are three or four small holes near the edge for fastening the doll onto a base. Half dolls were often sewed onto a shaped cushion and dressed in Colonial costume, to be used as pincushions. In the 1920's they were often turned into boudoir dolls, or they topped quite decorative telephone covers. Sad to say, half dolls were sometimes even made into lamp shades, over a flaring wire frame.

It seems best to treat half dolls just as if they were full-length dolls, and to dress them as *dolls*. First, make a stuffed-cloth base in the right proportions and sew the doll onto it. Then dress it in a full-skirted costume. If the arms are well shaped, give the doll short puff sleeves and a low-necked bodice.

Half dolls often turn up in thrift shops. A little cleaning and minor repairing will make them worthy of a place in your collection.

We can't possibly mention all materials dollmakers have ever used, but celluloid deserves special attention, because it's an ancestor of modern plastics.

About 1856, a man named Alexander Parkes made the first celluloid, in England. Then, in 1869, an American, John Wesley Hyatt, who was trying to find a substitute for ivory, discovered how to make celluloid commercially. Finally in 1880, the Celluloid Manufacturing Company was formed in Newark, New Jer-

Turn half dolls into full-length dolls by sewing them to base, dressing like other dolls. In center is typical half doll before assembling. All three dolls have real hair.

Three modern celluloid dolls. Small doll in center is unusually fine, has dimpled body, well-painted features, flat-heeled feet. Larger dolls have clothes crocheted from wool yarn.

sey, and began to make celluloid dolls under two U.S. patents. The formula used for making celluloid called for a mixture of gum camphor, dissolved in alcohol, to which was added dry gun cotton. This was rolled, heated, and put under pressure, then made into flat sheets that could be cut and placed into molds for shaping.

German manufacturers quickly entered the picture and made vast numbers of dolls and toys from celluloid. They marked their exports with a mark soon to become famous — a tiny raised tortoise, sometimes enclosed in a diamond-shaped frame, and often with the words, *Schutze-Marke* (protected trademark). Sometimes there were also numbers, giving the size, and always after 1891, the word *Germany*.

Many of the molds used for making bisque dolls were also used for those of celluloid. The George Borgfeldt Company of New York sent special molds to Germany to be made into celluloid heads. This company was the same one that assembled Bye-Lo dolls which they had imported from Germany, so it is possible that this is why so many Bye-Los, even with bisque heads, have celluloid hands marked with the tortoise.

Beautiful celluloid dolls were made in all European countries, as well as in the United States, and finally in Japan. Even though plastic is now crowding out celluloid, the older material is still plentiful. In fact, the little modern celluloid doll in the illustration was bought recently in a chain-store toy department for less than 50 cents, and it's of good quality material and workmanship.

The quality of celluloid doll heads depends almost entirely on the quality of the molds, because celluloid is so plastic that it duplicates every detail of the mold.

Celluloid has several good qualities: 1) it's lightweight, 2) has a smooth surface, 3) is washable, 4) can be given a lifelike color, and 5) ages to a soft mellow ivory tint. It also has some bad points: 1) it's highly inflammable, 2) in its lighter weights it will sometimes crack, and 3) its colors tend to fade.

Another material which was first used hundreds of years ago in the making of dolls is metal. The first metal dolls were made in Europe during the Middle Ages from gold and silver as charms, or from lead and tin as toy soldiers — which of course are really dolls.

About 1850, English doll manufacturers used metal as a base for wax doll heads, and the Springfield, Vermont, dollmakers put

Little Boy Blue, Little Miss Muffet, and Bo-Peep have cornhusk bodies, clothes; cornsilk hair. Their wire frames are bendable.

metal hands and feet on many of their wooden dolls. Climaxing it all, a patent was taken out in 1887 for making doll heads from sheets of brass, tin, or zinc and riveting or soldering them together. They were finished with enamel, just as papier-mâché heads were painted. The most common of these metal heads were the Minerva and the Juno, both made in the form of heads, to be attached to sawdust-filled cloth or leather bodies. Some of these dolls were made with painted hair, and others wore curly wigs. Some had inset glass eyes, and others had painted eyes. Many had closed mouths; others were open-mouthed, with little teeth.

Metal dolls are rated as secondary collectors' items, and consequently their price is not too high. Every well-rounded collection should include one, because metal has shared in the long search, still going on, for a dollmaking material that's durable, lifelike, and inexpensive.

The ancestors of Pocahontas probably played with cornhusk dolls, because corn was native to this hemisphere, and cornhusks and dolls go together just as perfectly as dolls and little girls. Our pioneers made cornhusk dolls for their children in the same way that people still make them in the mountains of the South. The cornhusk dolls shown in this chapter came from West Virginia, and the people who made them put a lot of humor into the little hillbillies. They're so easy to make that it would be fun to follow the directions and make a few for your collection.

The only material you need is a handful of cornhusks. Soak the husks overnight in water, and then trim off the stiff ends and discolored places with scissors. Follow the directions given in the drawings. Do *not* use glue or cement; fasten the parts together with fine strips of cornhusk torn about one-half inch wide.

When the dolls are finished, mark their features with pen and ink. Tint their cheeks and lips with a small brush dipped in diluted food coloring. Some of the dolls in the picture have colors painted on their clothes, perhaps with dye or berry juice.

Houn' dogs and mules, as well as people, are fun to make of cornhusks.

Little Aunt Ackey represents another kind of primitive doll

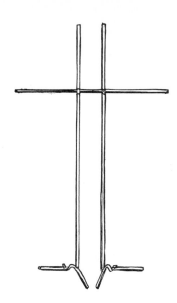

Twist pieces of light-
weight wire to form the
frame for cornhusk dolls
like West Virginians.

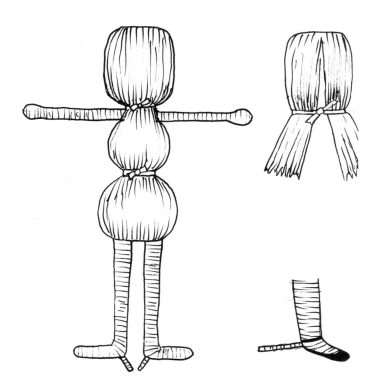

Details of cornhusk doll showing short pieces of wire at
heels, which enable dolls to stand. Upper right — One kind
of bonnet, to be tied in place by husk strip.

Miss Muffet has flowers painted on skirt
with dye or food color. Hair is cornsilk.

you can make for your collection. Get a medium-sized apple, a
package of pipe cleaners, and inch-wide strips of old nylon
stockings.

Peel the apple, remove the stem, and scoop a hole in the
blossom end just big enough to hold a 2-inch-long wooden dowel.

About halfway between stem and blossom ends, dig out two
round depressions for the eyes, carve a roughly shaped nose,
make a slit for the mouth, and trim the apple to make a knobby
chin. Don't try to get fine details — just the general planes of the
face.

Put the head in a warm place (the top of a radiator or water
heater) to dry for several weeks. As it dries, it will shrink and
grow brown.

For eyes, use white beads with dabs of black paint for pupils,
or use navy beans painted the same way. Cement the eyes in

place. Rub a dab of rouge on each cheek, and color the mouth with diluted food coloring. Now brush the entire head with one coat of lacquer or clear varnish. When it's dry, cement the head onto the wooden dowel.

Make the body of pipe cleaners and coil them around the dowel at the neck. Wrap the body with strips of nylon hose, covering the wire smoothly. If you want to model hands and feet, put papier mâché directly onto the wrapped wire. When the papier mâché dries, cover it with oil paint tinted to match the color of the face.

You can make a good wig from gray mercerized darning cotton. Follow the instructions for wigs in the rag-doll chapter, but cut the pieces of darning cotton long enough to coil into a bun at the back of the head. Fasten it in place with short stitches of the darning cotton.

Little Aunt Ackey has pipe-cleaner body, dried-apple head. Wind her body with strips of nylon hose to make skirt and shawl. She can hold or carry a bag or basket.

Upper left — Old shell doll from Brittany has papier-mâché head, hands, leather-brimmed hat. She's about 8 inches tall. Right — Doll made all of shells is 7 inches tall. Bottom — Miniature all-shell doll, 2 inches tall. Parasol is shell cemented to fish rib. Made by Laytons, Florida.

Because of their realistic wrinkles, apple dolls should always represent old people. Alice Daye, famous for her apple dolls, made dozens of them — no two alike. Kimport once listed some of them: an old country doctor and his elderly patient, an old shoemaker puffing on his pipe, a banjo player tapping his foot to the music, a hobo, and a group of apple-vendor dolls whose hands were also made of dried apples, representing Oregon, the apple state.

If you live by the ocean, you have probably already tried to make dolls of either kelp or sea shells. Shells vary so much in size, color, and shape that it's impossible to give you exact plans and drawings for turning them into dolls. Just gather the shells and let your imagination go to work.

One method for fastening the shells together is to make a paper cone the height of the doll's body and stuff it full of paper to hold it in shape. Using this base for support, cement the shells together with white glue or airplane cement. Use plenty of glue, but try to have all the excess run down behind the shells where it won't show. When the cement is thoroughly dry, remove the paper cone.

Shell dolls are strictly for collectors, and aren't to be played with. The ones shown here will give you a few ideas for making your own.

Many beautiful dolls being made today will someday be just as highly prized by collectors as are any dolls of the past. It's not the purpose of this book to describe them; all we can do is urge you to take care of every doll you own, so that some day in the future you'll be able to look at your dolls and recall happy memories.

9

How To Dress Your Dolls

Doll collectors often divide their enthusiasm so evenly between dolls and their love of dressing them that it's hard to decide which comes first. If you have never dressed a doll, why not discover for yourself which side of collecting is the most fun for *you?*

There are a few rules that doll dressmakers should always follow. First, a doll's clothes should be in keeping with its age and character. For example, an old wooden or rag doll should never wear the clothes of a 20th century debutante. A baby doll would look pathetic in grownup clothes. An antique doll should always wear old-fashioned materials, while modern dolls should be dressed in crisp, new fabrics. This rule, of course, doesn't apply to costume and character dolls; their clothes should be in keeping with their place in history or the people they represent.

Watch a doll lover when she examines a doll. She almost always looks first at the underwear. This means that a doll's lingerie is just as important as its outer garments, and that the time you spend on making tiny tucks or sewing on lace will not be wasted.

It's a good idea to make doll clothes with either buttons and buttonholes, snap fasteners, or hooks and eyes. Then it's easier to remove them for cleaning. Both dolls and their clothes do get dirty.

For making doll clothes, use only the finest, softest materials. If the cloth is figured, choose small designs in scale with the size of the doll. Lace should be lacy and soft, and embroidered trimming always dainty and sheer.

Make doll clothes by hand instead of on the sewing machine, and take the smallest, most even stitches you possibly can. Use No. 60 or 70 thread and a fine needle. Try sewing with a fine crewel needle, for the eye is large enough to thread easily but won't leave ugly holes where you take the stitches.

As we said earlier, do learn to use a thimble when you sew, even if it seems awkward at first. It's much easier to give the needle a little push with a thimble than with your bare finger.

There are many commercial patterns for doll clothes, most of them in proportioned sizes for large dolls, which come with full instructions for putting them together. If you can find a pattern that will fit your doll, by all means use it. Then when you begin to make clothes for yourself, you'll discover that you already know how to read and follow a pattern's instructions.

Some dolls are either too large or too small for ready-made patterns, so you'll have to make your own. This isn't hard to do, even for a beginner.

Pattern books in the stores are just like libraries of modern styles, and it's a good idea to look through them and sketch clothes that appeal to you when you plan your own patterns.

But if your doll is to wear clothes of some other period, consult illustrated costume books at the library. Several of them show both historical and foreign dress. Also, look through the library's picture file, or in back issues of the *National Geographic Magazine*. Most of these illustrations are in full color, clearly printed and, of course, absolutely authentic. Pictures in children's fairy tales and storybooks are also helpful, and don't forget reproductions of paintings in books on art.

Once you've decided on a dress style, draw an outline of your doll on a piece of paper, and take its measurements at the places shown here on the chart. Jot them down on the outline. Your pattern will be a combination of these measurements and the basic pattern shown in the illustration. Allow about ½ inch extra width on each side seam so the clothes won't be too tight. In addition, allow ⅛ inch extra for the seams. It's a good idea to make patterns for underclothes and to cut out, fit, and finish the panties and slip before you draft the pattern for a dress. Then you can make allowance for the bulk of the undergarments.

Therefore, as soon as you've cut the patterns for the panties and slip, pin them onto the doll at the seam lines to test the fit. If you make the patterns of tissue paper, you'll find it easy to do this because the paper is pliable and soft and will cling together during the fitting. If you find that the pattern is right, mark it and put it aside while you make the next pattern. If the pattern doesn't fit, change it until it's perfect. It takes only a moment to verify a pattern this way so you won't waste time and material in making a garment that doesn't fit.

Once you have accurate slip and pantie patterns, smooth out the material you've chosen, working on a table or counter. Lawn, dimity, organdy, sheer nylon, or rayon are all suitable materials for making these garments. Fold it double, and pin the pattern in place. Cut out the garment with smooth, even snips of the scissors so there will be no uneven edges.

Baste the pieces together at the seams and sew them ⅛ inch from the edge, making tiny straight stitches. Fasten the thread securely at the end of each seam. It's best to make French seams if the material is likely to ravel or is quite sheer. Most seams are finished simply by pinking the edges, with either pinking shears or regular scissors. The illustration shows both methods.

After the underwear is all finished, leave it on the doll and measure for the dress or outer garments, again using the chart and your basic measurements as a guide. Fit the dress pattern, and make whatever corrections are needed, just as you corrected the underwear patterns. Cut out the dress and join the seams just as you did those of the panties and slip.

The drawing shows how to finish skirt and sleeve bands, how

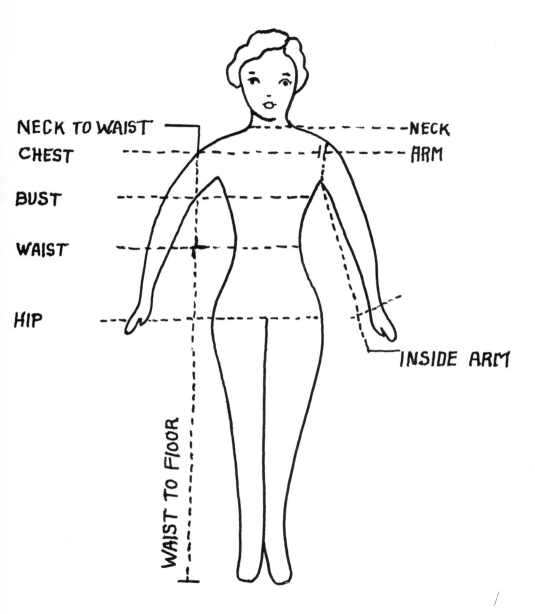

NECK TO WAIST
CHEST
BUST
WAIST
HIP

NECK
ARM

INSIDE ARM

WAIST TO FLOOR

Measurement chart for making doll clothes.

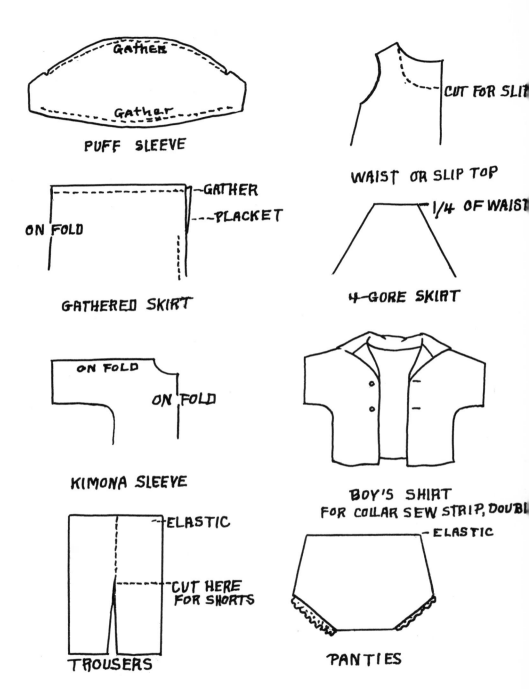

PUFF SLEEVE

WAIST OR SLIP TOP

GATHERED SKIRT

4-GORE SKIRT

KIMONA SLEEVE

BOY'S SHIRT
FOR COLLAR SEW STRIP, DOUBL

TROUSERS

PANTIES

Basic patterns for making doll clothes.

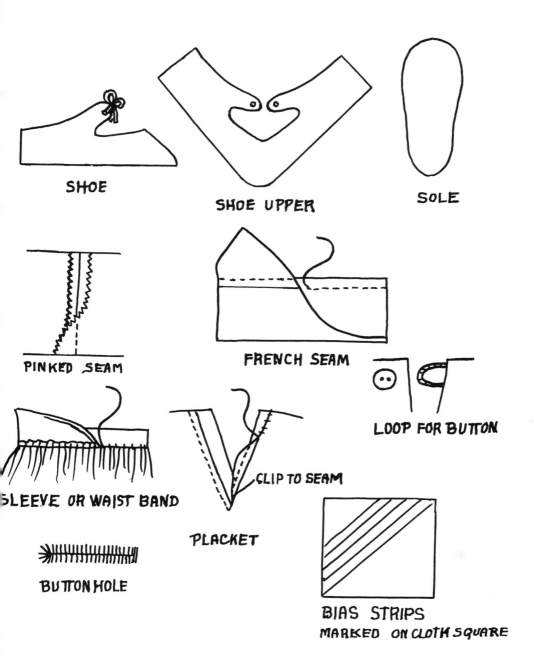

SHOE

SHOE UPPER

SOLE

PINKED SEAM

FRENCH SEAM

LOOP FOR BUTTON

SLEEVE OR WAIST BAND

PLACKET

CLIP TO SEAM

BUTTON HOLE

BIAS STRIPS
MARKED ON CLOTH SQUARE

Sewing details for making doll clothes.

to make a placket, how to cut bias strips for binding neck edges, how to make a loop for a button, and how to make buttonholes. Work neatly and don't try to hurry. If you make a mistake, pull out the stitches and correct the error.

"Oh, it's good enough," is no way for a doll dressmaker to talk.

Paris dress designers often work without patterns and pin dress material directly onto the persons who are to wear the clothes. After you have had a little practice with patterns, try this method for making your doll clothes. Turn the cloth *wrong side out,* pin it in place, snip and trim carefully until the dress fits, and then remove it and baste it together where the pins were. Sew the seams together and finish the dress neatly.

In an earlier chapter, we talked about half dolls. Molly, the beautiful Colonial lady shown here, is a full doll, but is dressed exactly as half dolls are dressed. If you have a doll whose head and arms are in good condition, but who is minus a leg or foot, salvage it by dressing it this way.

One of the pictures shows a doll I once made and dressed in a copy of a square-dance dress I was fond of. She wears her hair just as I did at the time, and her shoes are like those I wore with the dress. It's fun to do this same thing, dressing a doll in a copy of your confirmation dress, graduation dress, bridesmaid's dress, or your older sister's wedding gown. You'll have a permanent record of a great event, and you'll enjoy the doll more and more as time goes on.

My Scottish doll has many warm personal memories for me. He wears the tartan of the clan of my ancestors, which I found pictured in a tiny book of Scottish tartans. (A tartan is what is commonly called a plaid, and each clan had its own.) The same book describes the way kilts should be made, including overlap and correct length. Dugald MacDonald wears a Glengarry bonnet with a sprig of white heather stuck into its ribbon cockade. The brooch, or cairngorm, on his shoulder which holds his plaidie is made of five buttons, cemented one on top of the other, and the buttons on his black leather shoes (made from the lining of an old purse) are old cut-steel buckles found in a collection of buttons. My son cut apart the top frame of a small change purse and

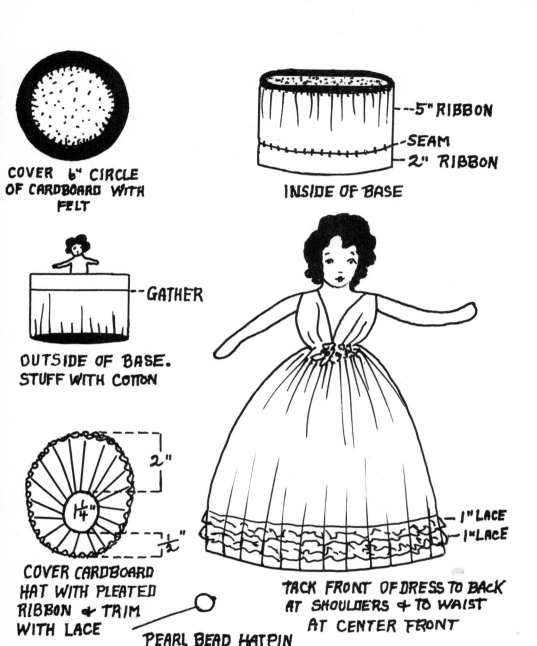

COVER 6" CIRCLE
OF CARDBOARD WITH
FELT

INSIDE OF BASE

--5" RIBBON

SEAM

2" RIBBON

GATHER

OUTSIDE OF BASE.
STUFF WITH COTTON

2"

1¼"

½"

COVER CARDBOARD
HAT WITH PLEATED
RIBBON & TRIM
WITH LACE

PEARL BEAD HATPIN

1" LACE

1" LACE

TACK FRONT OF DRESS TO BACK
AT SHOULDERS & TO WAIST
AT CENTER FRONT

Molly's an 8-inch celluloid doll; cotton-stuffed skirt's covered with satin,
lace. Dress, hat are new or scrap ribbon. *Courtesy Molly Yax.*

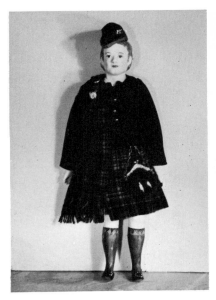

Helen herself in copy of favorite dress. Dress-
alike dolls are records of styles, materials.

Dugald MacDonald is future heirloom. Cos†
is authentic, even to heather sprig in bo◊

resoldered the hinges so that it would fit the top of the little fur
sporran, or pouch. I made the two little tails by tightly twisting
wisps of cotton and cementing them invisibly in the fur. The first
Dugald lived in the time of Bonnie Prince Charlie, on the Isle of
Skye. He's a man's doll, for Malcolm to pass on to his own son
someday.

Dollmakers are often asked to do unusual things, as once happened when a farmer's wife in the Middle West sent me a picture
of her little daughter and asked me to make a doll which would
be a "look-alike." She also sent scraps of material from one of the
little girl's dresses to use in dressing the doll. She closed her letter by saying, "I'll pay you, but I can't till the cow's had her calf.
I'm depending on that money for this present for my little girl."
She was as good as her word.

Use the suggestions in this chapter and practice dressing dolls
until you're an expert. Then pass along the word that you'll
dress dolls for other people. You can also make dresses for Christmas dolls, dress dolls for children in hospitals and institutions,
dress dolls for bazaars and sales, and dress dolls for yourself, just
for fun.

10

Repair Sick Dolls

The doll had no name when she came to me with the following note: "I am mailing you a — mercy, don't call it a gift, and don't be insulted, but it was a good Mexican doll, made by the artist who did them with the open mouth and teeth in the cloth faces, and inset eyes. This one is hopelessly battered, however, I know you are a good fixer-upper. Don't bother to return it if you don't want it — just drop in the incinerator."

Mrs. McKim knew very well that the nameless doll, wreck though she was, was not incurably ill, even though one arm was gone, her nose was mashed flat, and her only garment, a cotton skirt, covered a cloth body that was faded and worn.

Following good hospital procedure, the nameless doll was given a thorough, soapy bath. In fact she was scrubbed with a brush, rinsed, and washed again. After a final rinsing she was suspended by a string around her neck and hung to dry in the garage, where she looked more like the victim of a Western hanging than a doll on her way to a new life. By the time she was thoroughly dry, she looked even worse than she had before her bath, but at least she was clean.

Her body was made of tan-colored cotton cloth, much like percale, so it was easy to find a small piece of new material to use in replacing her missing arm. I made a pattern by holding her right arm down on a piece of paper and drawing around it, then adding the width of a seam. Two identical pieces were cut from the new cloth, stitched together, stuffed with cotton, then sewed into place on her shoulder.

When I started to operate on her poor, dilapidated head, I learned several surprising things about dollmaking. The first incision was to cut the black-yarn stitches that held her wig to her cloth head. The wig, made of yarn strands, was tacked to a folded square of black crinoline. It was in good condition, so I laid it to one side while the rest of the head was being worked on.

By this time, it was plain that the nameless doll suffered from severe internal injuries, and that it would be a good idea to make a record of her operation as I went along, so I wouldn't forget how she was put together. Perhaps some of this information would be useful in repairing or making other dolls. So a pencil and paper went to the operating table.

The doll's cloth head was joined to the body, but it was only the back part of a head. Her face — from the hairline, around the back of her ears, and under her chin to her neck — was a sort of mask covered with cloth. This cloth was a tightly stretched square, seamed up the back of the head, and hemmed at the base of the throat to the stuffed body. Tiny slits had been cut in the cloth covering for eyes, nostrils and mouth. After this covering had been traced on my chart as a record, it was discarded.

Removing the doll's "skin" uncovered the brown beeswax mask that formed her face. No wonder her nose was flat — the wax was broken and crumbling. There was no way to repair it, so she'd need a new mask. Perhaps the eyes and teeth could be set in it.

What do you suppose the eyes turned out to be, once they were dug out of the wax? Two white beans! The kind used for baked beans. A dot of black paint was the pupil of each eye. The five little pearly teeth turned out to be five little white beads strung on a fine wire and the ends of the wire pushed into the

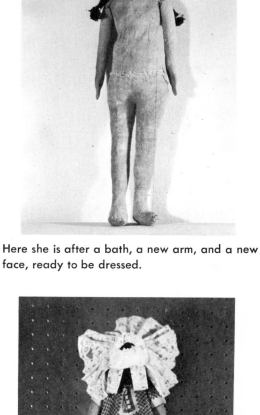

apidated doll before repairs. Dirty and with- an arm, it looked hopeless.

Here she is after a bath, a new arm, and a new face, ready to be dressed.

ne — Casilda — completes transformation. costume's traditional in Tehuantepec, Mex-

Back of Casilda's lace head covering shows the historic baby-dress sleeves and lace ruffles.

wax. What a clever person the maker of this doll must have been to think of using these simple, at-hand things to get the effect she wanted.

By this time, I was burning with curiosity to see what the doll's stuffing could be. Surely nothing as uninteresting as cotton or sawdust. Truly ingenious, the artist again used material I had never thought of: coarse, dry grass tightly packed. It was light-weight, smooth, and hadn't cost a peso, or even a centavo.

I made a new mask for the doll, exactly the size of the old one, but clay instead of wax. This was fired in a kiln, then painted with tempera paint to match the color of the body. The eyes and mouth were painted with tempera, and a little red was rubbed onto the doll's cheeks. Then the entire face was given a final coat of clear lacquer. The lacquer used in model making is just right for painting jobs this size, and is available in all model and hobby shops.

After the face mask had been cemented to the cloth part of the head, I painted the entire body with brown tempera paint. This cleared up her complexion problems and gave her a skin you didn't hate to touch. Her wig was sewed back just as it had been before. She lifted her head proudly now, even though she wore no clothes, and suddenly she became Casilda — no longer a nameless waif. The hospital dismissed her after a final checkup. She was well.

There was no way to find the name of Casilda's Mexican birth-place, but her stately posture suggested that it could only have been Tehuantepec. This is the city in which the regal-looking women overshadow their husbands and run their families and businesses while the men stay home or work in the fields. Tehu-antepec, on the Gulf of Mexico, has a colorful history, and the traditional costume of its strong, clever women is connected with it.

A legend says that many years ago a ship from Europe was wrecked off the nearby coast. In its hold it had carried a ship-ment of convent-made baby dresses, and when they washed up onto the beach, the Tehuanas promptly took possession of them.

The dresses were long, lace-trimmed and ruffled, and the women at once put them onto their heads, turning them into head-dresses. Ever since, the flaring head covering of Tehuantepec women includes all the parts of a baby dress, even the tiny sleeves. The photograph of Casilda's back shows this.

Another Tehuantepec legend has it that during the California gold rush in 1849, some of the ships carrying gold-seekers cut hundreds of miles from their voyage around the Horn and let passengers off at Tehuantepec. After crossing the Isthmus of Tehuantepec, the travelers picked up another ship, on the Pacific side of Mexico. For their transit, payment was made in gold coins. The women saved these big, shining gold pieces and strung them onto their necklaces. Ever since, these strings of gold coins have been handed down from one generation to another as cherished heirlooms, although their origin is almost forgotten.

Our Casilda wears her gold pieces, too, even though they're imitation coins made of chocolate wrapped in gold foil. They're so real looking and seemed to belong with her costume so much that I took a chance on their being well wrapped in foil and so wouldn't melt. After all, chocolate comes from Mexico, too.

It's fitting that Casilda should occupy so much space in this chapter, for she combines many of the things this book has stressed. Dolls are related to history, geography, costume, folk-lore and man's ingenuity. Best of all, Casilda's a reminder of the friendliness of doll collectors. What if she had been burned instead of rescued!

Years ago, when I was a beginner at dollmaking, someone sent me a beautiful, big china doll head to be repaired. One shoulder had been broken at the base of the neck, and the front of the chest was shattered. Sadly, I had to return it, for I didn't know about Durham's Water Putty, as I do now. This material does not shrink, dries as hard as stone, and can be painted. It is mixed with water. Hardware and paint stores sell it.

If that same doll came today for repairs, I should make them this way:

First fill the inside of the shoulders with non-hardening

clay, duplicating the unbroken side, bringing the clay only to the lower edge of the china so the entire edge of the missing part is exposed. Mix water putty with water according to directions on the can, so that it's the consistency of regular putty. Pack it smoothly on top of the clay the thickness of the china, joining it smoothly with the china. If there's to be a hole in the bottom of the shoulder to match one on the unbroken side, carefully make one now with a nail or wood splinter. Make the putty surface as smooth as possible and let it dry 24 hours. That's one advantage of this putty: It dries rather slowly, not like plaster of Paris. When it's dry, sandpaper it with fine sandpaper. Once in a while the putty refuses to stick to a china surface. If so, apply white glue to the joining, and let it dry well before going ahead. When the water putty is dry, remove the clay from the inside of the shoulder.

Paint the repaired place with white enamel paint. If the china is not a dead white, tint the paint with a dab of ultramarine oil paint until it matches. If the china head is flesh color, tint the white paint with a bit of red oil paint and a speck of yellow. If there's a slightly brownish cast to the color, add a tiny amount of blue. Brush this paint on smoothly.

If the surface isn't quite as glossy when dry as the original china, cover it with a coat of clear nail polish or model lacquer.

Even if the replaced part isn't exactly the same as the original head, a strong repair job will sometimes make it possible to salvage an otherwise good doll and cover the mended place with the dress. As an example, the doll I've just been discussing could have worn a high-necked dress to conceal the repairs, and she was an unusually sad case.

In an earlier chapter, I described several ways to make doll wigs. There is a way to make a wig of real hair. It's not difficult but does require a little patience.

Most dolls with wigs are made with fully shaped heads to which the wig is glued. Some older dolls, particularly German bisques, were made with open heads, especially the dolls with sleeping eyes. The kind of wig described here may be used on either kind of head. Briefly, it's a kind of cap to which hair is fastened and which is put on the doll head after being completed.

Many doll wigs are made of what is called mohair, a material that's sold by the yard at doll hospitals and supply houses offering doll-repair merchandise.

You can also use real human hair for making doll wigs. Buy an inexpensive switch of hair from a dime store, or ask a beauty operator to save you a handful of long trimmings. The hair should be at least 6 inches long for small dolls, and longer for large dolls. If you save the hair that's cut off when you part with your pony tail, you'll be able to use it for a wig that will be even more interesting to you in the future than it is now.

Whatever the source of the hair for a wig, the first step in making one is to fit the doll's head with a tight-fitting skull cap. Cut a circle of crinoline— black for a brunette, white for a blonde — which is large enough to cover the top of the head from the forehead to the hairline in back, just above the ears. Soak this circle in water, then dip it in stiff starch. While it's still wet, smooth it down over the doll's head, stretching it and molding it in place. Let it dry on the head.

Measure the outer edge of this circle around the back of the head from one ear to the other. Cut a piece of silk seam binding, the color of the hair, about one inch longer than this distance. Thumbtack this strip of tape down onto a piece of tissue paper and place tiny bundles of hair across it. Use strands of hair twice the length the wig is to be and center them on the tape. Spread the hair evenly the length of the tape. Cover it with a strip of tissue paper and stitch through the hair and both layers of paper. It's best to do this stitching on a sewing machine, setting it for a close stitch and using thread the same color as the hair. Pull off both pieces of tissue paper.

Fold the tape in half and thumbtack it down at each end, which will form a fringe. Cover the fold with another strip of tissue paper. Stitch through both paper and hair, close to the fold. Pull off the paper.

Cement this strip close to the edge of the crinoline cap and

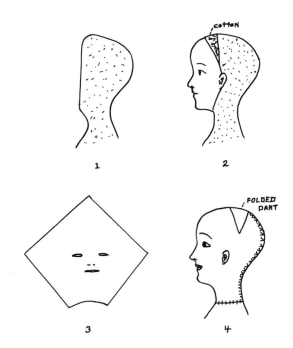

Doll head with mask face. 1) Cut back of head, stuff
with cotton; 2) cement wax or clay mask to cloth,
fill between with cotton; 3) cloth with slits is stretched
over head; 4) cloth after fitting, sewing.

allow it to dry. This one strip of fringe is enough for a wig for a
small doll. Larger dolls may require two or more strips of fringe,
about ½ inch apart.

For the top of the head, measure a strip of tape the length of
the crown of the head to the forehead. Spread bundles of hair
across the tape just as you did for the fringe. Repeat the line of
stitching you made before, then tear off the paper. Make an
invisible part by spreading the hair on each side of the stitching
to the opposite side, just as you'd interlace your fingers. Cement
this strip onto the crinoline cap from the crown of the head to
the front edge of the cap. Tie the head and wig in a kerchief
until the cement is dry.

Spread glue on the inside of the crinoline cap and replace it on
the doll head. Tie it in place again until it dries. This type of wig
may be brushed, if done carefully. Or it may be curled. Heat an
ice pick or curling iron and test it on a piece of white cloth to

make sure it is not too hot, then wind strands of the hair over it and hold in place for a few seconds.

Quite often the only repair needed for a doll is the replacement of a wig, and this is the easiest way to make one at home.

Another common complaint among sick dolls is the loss of a finger or toe, sometimes even an entire hand or foot. Here again, use water putty. This applies to either china or composition doll bodies. First brush the holding surface with white glue; while it's still damp, model the new part directly on the doll. After the putty dries, match the body color and paint the new part as described before.

The condition is more serious when an entire arm or leg is missing. Before you decide to make a new limb, see whether you can find a doll with similar parts in a thrift or salvage shop. If not, you may want to model a new arm or leg, duplicating the one already attached to the doll. Use the following mixture:

1 cup flour
½ cup salt
3 teaspoons powdered alum
About ½ cup water

Mix this to the consistency of stiff dough, and after the new part is dry, paint it to match the doll.

There are two schools of thought about doll repairing. Some perfectionists want every doll to look just like new; some sentimentalists insist that every mark of time and use should be preserved. My own feeling is that when a doll has some special importance or association, it should be left as it is. But when it will benefit by careful repairs, they should be made. Just make sure that the character of the doll isn't lost.

As with Casilda, start with a thorough cleaning. Sometimes this is the only thing needed. Dirt covers many beautiful dolls in a way that makes them appear hopeless until they've had a bath. Soap and water are safe for china, celluloid, and composition dolls. For wax dolls it's safer to use liquid wax or a little cold cream. Apply this cautiously, because it would be a pity to cut through the body color. Small cracks may often be repaired by smoothing the edges together with a warm (not hot) knife.

It's easy to replace small parts on celluloid dolls with water putty, then paint them with enamel in the body color and finish the surface with clear lacquer.

Even doll-hospital surgeons shake their heads and refuse to operate on dolls made of the modern soft, lifelike rubber or plastic materials. If such a doll has particularly dear memories for you and you can't bear to throw it away, you might follow a suggestion once made by Mildred Chafey in *Doll Talk*. She salvages dolls of this type by first securing cracked or broken necks to the body, and sealing cracks together with strips of adhesive tape. She then makes a close-fitting cover for the body of heavy unbleached muslin, to which she sews fitted tights covering

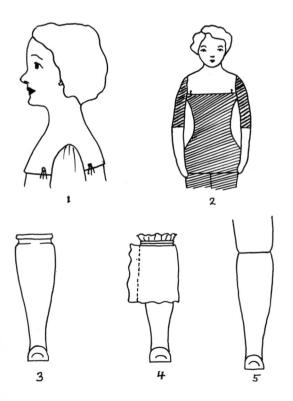

1) Fastening china head to cloth body with heavy thread through holes in head's lower edge; 2) cloth doll with china head, arms, and legs; arms and legs sewed in cloth casing; 3) china leg has groove at top; 4) slip into cloth section and wrap tightly with thread; 5) turn cloth right side out and stuff with sawdust.

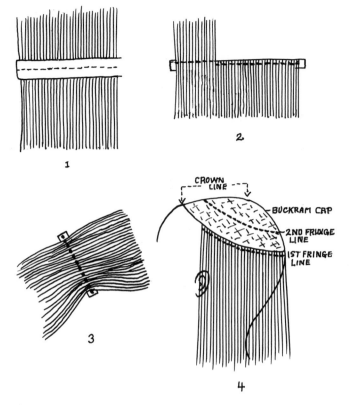

Wig of human hair. 1) Spread hair along strip of tape, cover with strip of tissue paper, stitch through all three layers on sewing machine, then pull off paper; 2) turn one side of hair down at stitching and stitch again, close to fold; 3) make crown section as you did fringe, turn under ends of tape, and cement to head after fringe is in place; 4) place on buckram cap to fasten strips of hair fringe. Curl or braid hair after cement is dry.

arms and legs. Although this is a makeshift method, it will at least protect a precious doll that can't be repaired any other way.

Following are a few miscellaneous suggestions you may find helpful.

• When a doll's dress is in good condition except for fading, carefully rip the seams, turn the sections, and restitch the seams and hem. You don't have to be an experienced dressmaker to do this.

- If the dress is in tatters, rip it apart and use the pieces for a pattern. Preferably, use new material as nearly like the original as possible.
- Old wigs may be safely cleaned by dipping them in cleaning solvent.
- When cloth or leather bodies need mending, cover rips and holes with small neat patches sewed or cemented in place. If some of the stuffing has been lost, replace it with cotton or sawdust before applying the patch.
- When you make drastic repairs on a doll, take time to write down, in order, each step you take, just as I did when rebuilding Casilda. Even the best memory can fail.
- The drawing shows how to sew cloth parts to china arms and legs, and also how to fasten china heads to cloth bodies. This is the method used in assembling the china dolls of the past, and is easier than it looks.
- Jointed dolls, especially those with composition bodies and china or bisque heads, have a common complaint. Sooner or later, the elastic that holds them together will stretch and lose its snap, and must be replaced. The only tools you need for doing this are a pair of small pliers and a long crochet hook. Buy enough round elastic (the thickness of a match) to reach, doubled, from the doll's neck to its knees and from one wrist to the other. Follow the chart, starting at the wire hook inside one knee. Loop the elastic through this hook and pull it up through the leg parts with the crochet needle, through the body and arm and the hook at the neck, then down the other side of the doll. Tighten it as firmly as possible, then tie the ends of the elastic together at the other knee.

Cut another length of elastic and loop it over the hook of the hand, then pull it doubled up the arm and across the chest to the other arm. Do not pass through the neck hook. Run the elastic down the other arm and tighten and tie it at the other hand hook. It's important to pull the elastic as tightly as possible so the body won't sag at the joints.

110

Restringing dolls for other doll owners is another way to make your hobby pay for itself. It's not difficult; it's simply a matter of doing something that other people won't bother to do for themselves. And that's really the theme of this entire chapter.

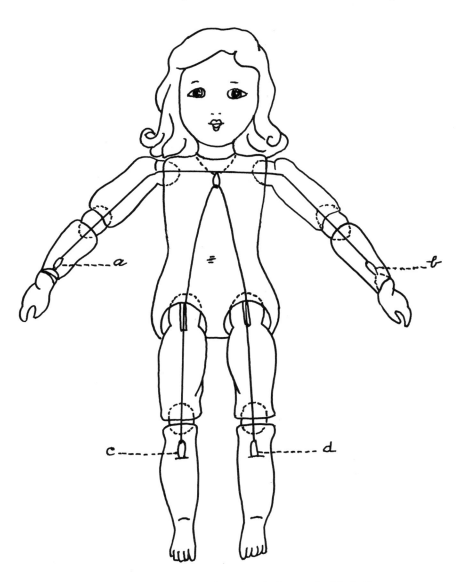

Restringing jointed doll: Use 2 lengths of elastic, doubled. Run one from a to b, other from c to d. Tighten before tying. The only tool needed is a long crochet hook.

11

Dolls Live Here

Flora Gill Jacobs, in her book, *A History of Doll Houses*, tells us we should say *dollhouse*, not doll's house. Perhaps that rule was made by people who think a house can only belong to someone who is alive, and that dolls are not alive. Some people claim that when no one is looking, dolls really *do* come alive and give parties and move furniture in the houses they live in. So perhaps we just think that dolls are not alive. It's fun to pretend, and that's why dollhouses are such fun.

The little girl who owned Racketty-Packetty house also owned another dollhouse, Tidy Castle. But who nowadays has room for even one big house for dolls, much less two? Folding dollhouses are made, and they're better than nothing, but it's far better to keep a house set up all the time, with the furniture in place. A dollhouse is also a good place to display your doll collection. I'll talk more about that in the next chapter.

Most dollhouses not only require quite a lot of floor or table space, but also are furnished with Colonial or Victorian period furniture. The house shown here corrects both situations, for it's made to be hung on the wall, just like a hanging shelf, and it's designed to be decorated in contemporary style. Call it an apartment, a vacation cabin, or a two-story house. It has a flight of stairs, but it's a dollhouse at its simplest. It's only 11 inches wide and about 20 inches long, yet it has a living area, a kitchenette, bath, and bedroom.

Boys like to make model planes and cars. With the same materials, girls can make a house and its furniture for their dolls. There's no reason why girls shouldn't learn to use simple tools; in fact, there's every reason that they should. This dollhouse was made in our kitchen from an apple box and scraps of balsa and plywood. It's put together with white glue and small finishing nails. It was painted with oil stain and model lacquer. The only tools used were a handsaw, hammer, jackknife, and 12-inch ruler. In order to keep construction simple, the house has no windows and only one partition. If you need help in putting it together, call on a hammer-and-saw veteran, but don't stand by and let him do the work. Have him show you how; then do it yourself.

Most dollhouse furniture is made in the scale of 1 inch to 1 foot, which means that a dollhouse man would be about 6 inches tall, and his wife 5½ inches. Dollhouse dolls should be more slender than other dolls. The basic rule for dollhouses, furniture and dolls is to keep them all in proportion. That will make them seem to be more real.

Most dollhouse furniture in the stores is made of plastic, but except for the bathroom fixtures, we decided to make our own, using balsa wood, plywood, and various odds and ends I'll describe later. The set of bathroom pieces also included a baby's bathinette, which we took apart and used as a sink; a linen hamper, which was converted into a kitchen range; a dresser, which was lacquered and used in the bedroom; and an armless chair, which became a living-room chair. The only thing included in the set which we discarded was the frame for the bathinette. Actually, even the bathroom furnishings could have been made of balsa wood. We bought the plastic furniture before cutting the box, to be certain that it would be the right size.

The apple box was without a lid and had no center divider. After the paper labels were removed from the ends, the box was

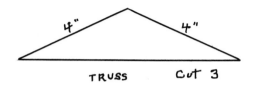

TRUSS   Cut 3

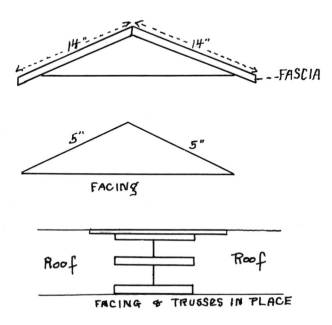

FASCIA

FACING

Roof   Roof

FACING & TRUSSES IN PLACE

Fasten roof parts together with glue, finishing nails.

turned on its side on the worktable, and all loose or projecting nails were pulled and thrown away. Then the work proceeded in the following order.

Carefully remove the top side of the box and set it aside until later. It will become the floor for the second story.

The height of the first-floor rooms is 6½ inches, floor to ceiling, so cut three ½-inch-wide strips of ¼-inch balsa wood to support the second floor. Apply white glue to these strips, and hold them in place with ½-inch wire brads. The top of the strips should be 6½ inches from the floor at the back and at both ends of the box.

In order to give the second story enough height, make an extension for the back of the box by cutting a triangular-shaped piece of ¼-inch plywood the length of the back and 4¼ inches above the balsa strip in the center. Join this piece to the top edge of the back by applying white glue to both edges. Cover the joint with a ½-inch strip of balsa wood, gluing it in place and fastening with wire brads.

Cut two risers for the stairs from ¼-inch-thick balsa wood, following the diagram. There will be 11 steps, so cut 11 treads from the ¼-inch balsa wood, making them each 1 inch wide and 2 inches long.

Cement and fasten with brads *one* of the risers to the back of the box, placing it 2 inches from the right-hand wall at the floor level, and 8⅜ inches from the right-hand wall just under the support strip.

Now take the top side of the box which is to be the floor of the second story and measure it carefully so it will fit inside the box. There are probably a few unsightly nail holes in this wood, so saw off the extra length by removing a strip from each end of the piece. If the side is in more than one piece, hold it together by gluing ½-inch balsa-wood strips to its under side. These pieces will look like ceiling beams.

Now cut out an oblong of wood from the back edge of the second floor, 3 inches long and 2½ inches wide. This will be the stairwell, and the left-hand edge of the opening should meet the edge of the top stair tread.

The only partition used in this dollhouse is the one between bedroom and bath. Cut it next, using ¼-inch plywood, and sawing it 8½ inches long at the floor and 7⅝ inches high. The bathroom is 4½ inches wide, so trim out a ¼-inch piece of the strip that covers the extension of the back wall. This allows the partition to fit snugly against the wall. Fasten the partition in place by driving three 1-inch finishing nails through the second-story floor board, covering the bottom of the partition with glue and pounding it onto the projecting nails.

Finish the stairs by gluing and fastening a tread onto each riser

115

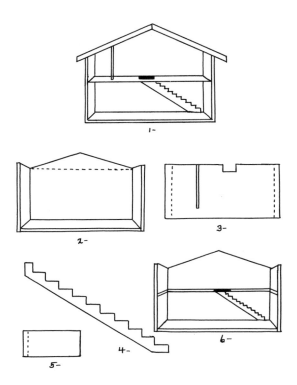

1) Completed dollhouse made from 11" x 19½" apple box; 2) roof extension in place on back wall; 3) second floor with stairwell cut out, partition added; 4) risers for stairway are cut from 1"-wide strips of balsa, notched to hold treads; 5) 11 treads formed from thin balsa are fastened to risers; 6) first stage of dollhouse is completed, ready to have second floor slipped inside and roof fastened to top.

with a ¼-inch wire brad. Cement the second riser to the floor and repeat the gluing and fastening of each tread, letting the ends of the treads project about ⅛ inch beyond the riser.

The floors of this dollhouse were covered with adhesive plastic covering, but as the material refuses to stick very tightly to rough wood, the edges were first brushed with white glue, then applied.

Tempera paint is the easiest material to use for painting the walls, although regular wall paint may be used. Paint the walls of both first and second floors next.

Now for the roof. Instead of supporting the roof with another partition, we used what builders call roof trusses. This makes the

116

roof entirely independent of the walls for strength, and is easy to make.

Cut 3 trusses from 1-inch-thick balsa wood, using the peak of the roof as your pattern. Make also, cut exactly the same, a facing for the front of the house by sawing ¼-inch plywood, with the grain of the wood going up and down.

Make two roof pieces by cutting ¼-inch plywood the width of the house and 4 inches longer than the distance from the peak of the roof to the outside wall. This will make an overhang. Bevel the inner edges of the two roof sections so they'll meet exactly at the roof peak. Glue each truss and fasten it with 1-inch finishing nails, through the roof and into the truss. Bring the roof sections close together at the top. The illustration shows this more clearly than words can describe it. Set the back truss about ½ inch in from the edge of the roof piece, and the center truss in the center of the roof sections. Nail and glue the plywood facing that you cut so that it's flush with the edge of the roof, and then glue and nail the front truss against it on the inside.

Allow the glue to dry thoroughly; then cement and nail the roof to the house.

Cover the entire roof with a thick coating of white glue, and sprinkle it with sawdust. Press the sawdust into the glue. After the glue dries, brush off excess sawdust.

The last thing to do is to glue a fascia over the front edge of the roof. Cut this out of ⅛-inch balsa wood the exact length of the projecting roof. Bevel the center edges.

Paint or stain the outside of the dollhouse, including the plywood facing and the fascia. Don't paint the surface of the roof.

Put two large screw eyes into the edges of the side walls, at the back, near the top. These will be used when you hang the dollhouse on the wall.

This completes the dollhouse, and now it's ready for decorating.

Since we bought the bathroom fixtures, it was easy to put them into place, using a little glue to hold them against the bathroom wall. A dime-store mirror was also glued to the wall above the wash basin.

In the hobby shop where we had bought the balsa wood and

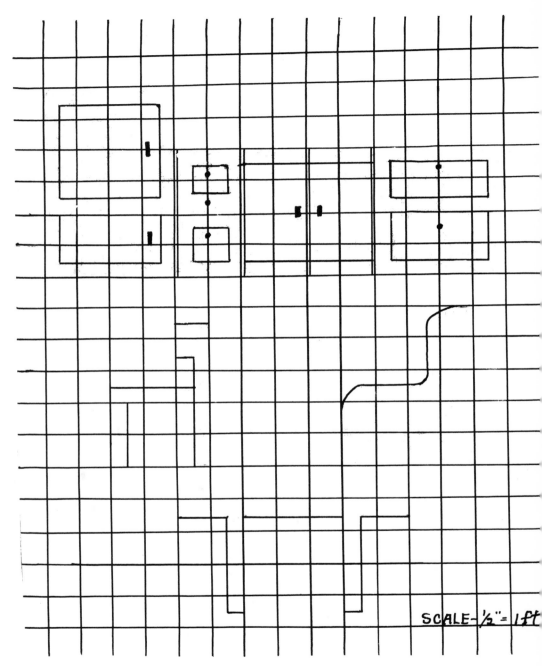

SCALE-½"= 1 ft

Diagrams for making dollhouse furniture.

Dollhouse doll on frame of pipe cleaners. Head is circle of pink cloth filled with cotton. Pipe cleaners are wound to waist with thread, wrapped with ½" strips of pink crepe paper. Pencil in features. Hair's embroidery floss.

tempera paint, we discovered pre-cut packages of short lengths of balsa wood in several thicknesses. For less than $1, we had enough material to make furniture for several dollhouses. Balsa is so soft it can be cut easily with a jackknife or single-edge razor blade (be careful of your fingers) and yet strong enough to use for dollhouse furniture.

The diagrams give patterns for a table, which can be changed easily into a stool or coffee table; a lounge chair, which can be used for making a sofa by fastening the ends shown to a flat piece of balsa; and for a kitchen cabinet. By the time you complete these pieces, you'll have learned enough to make others, copying real furniture or designing something new.

The drawers and doors on the refrigerator and cabinet were drawn on the balsa wood with a soft pencil by pressing it down hard. Then, after the piece was painted, the lines were retraced with a pencil. The handles are small staples pressed into the wood.

119

A heavy turkish toweling washcloth became both a bedroom rug and a bedspread, each piece fringed. Just for fun, we put a pair of curtains on the bedroom wall, using a piece of wire for a curtain rod, with a bead cemented to each end.

Plastic sponges make good upholstery pads and mattresses. A chrome-plated doorknob turned upside down was the foundation for a mosaic table. Tiny bits of colored glass cemented to the top made it look real. The Danish-type fireplace in the living room was once a spice can. Cutting off the bottom of the can and painting it black took just a few minutes. The picture on the wall was clipped from an advertisement. The artificial plant in the corner of the room was clipped from a spray of leaves we bought at our dime store and fastened into a tiny Mexican pottery cup.

There is no reason you can't furnish this same dollhouse with Early American, Colonial, Provincial, or Victorian furniture and accessories without making any changes in the house itself.

As for the dolls who live in it, the only thing to remember is that they should be in scale, just as much as the furniture is. Dollhouse dolls look more real if they are slimmer than other dolls of the same height. Even paper dolls would enjoy this house, and it would welcome them.

12

Share Your Dolls

If you have made every kind of doll described in this book, or even a few of them, you already have enough dolls to make an interesting display. If you are already a doll collector, do you have your dolls where they can be seen and enjoyed?

A collection is always an inspiration to other people and sometimes a surprise to those who have always thought that dolls were just children's toys, instead of being ageless records of history, worldwide in importance.

It's time to think of ways to display your dolls and of how to share your collection. And of course, you must first decide on a place to put them where they can be kept safe and clean, yet be seen. A case with a glass door is ideal, and one of the best types is an old-fashioned china cabinet, either built-in or movable. Equally good is a sectional bookcase with glass doors. An open bookcase is convenient, but the dolls will get dusty and aren't as safe as they would be behind glass.

Shadow boxes are close cousins of cabinets and cases but can be hung on the wall. Attach a shallow wooden box to the back of a large picture frame. Line the back of the box with velvet, if the doll is an elegantly dressed lady, or with burlap or grass cloth if she is the peasant type. After the doll is in place, seal the glass to the frame. You won't be able to take her out and hold her, but she'll be safe from dust. This is one of the best ways to protect a rare old doll.

Perhaps you'll want to make a more elaborate background — something that will be almost a picture. Have you ever seen a diorama? It's a three-dimensional scene in miniature, and could be adapted to displaying dolls. This also could be placed behind glass.

We have talked before about dolls and books. Why not scatter a few dolls between the books on your shelves? This is a good place to put character dolls: Alice in Wonderland, Heidi, Hansel and Gretel, Robinson Crusoe, and of course Raggedy Ann and Andy. If you don't have a doll to match your favorite book, why not get busy and make one? Foreign dolls belong here, too, and so do costume dolls.

Before you put dolls on display, write the name of the doll and its age, with interesting bits of information about it, on a slip of paper and pin it to her petticoat. In later years this will be of great value in establishing the doll's age and history. Let's hope that your dolls will live to be as old as Mother Parlington.

Patented metal stands are made for holding dolls upright. They are adjustable in height, and they have a round metal base and a wire loop to clasp around the doll's waist, under her clothes.

You can make effective doll stands at home by forming cones from stiff cardboard or thin tin or aluminum. Make the cone just large enough to reach from the doll's waist to its feet after the top is clipped off. Slip the doll's feet into the cone, and then fasten the cone edges together with masking tape. The doll's skirts will cover the cone.

A temporary stand can be made by tying a doll to a soft-drink bottle or milk carton, or by standing it in a jar or vase, letting the skirts cover the makeshift stand.

After you've fitted your dolls with stand-up equipment it's

time to think about arranging a doll show. The most obvious places are in schools or libraries, and here are a few suggestions.

An American-history class would be interested in seeing a display of dolls making maple sugar, building a log cabin, or having a quilting bee, a sleigh ride, or a barn raising. Dress the dolls in costumes copied from those in Currier and Ives prints or textbook illustrations.

Borrow a model-railroad layout and make men dolls of suitable size. Stand a few feminine passengers on the station platform, or let them sit in model automobiles, waiting for the train. As a class project, this would interest both boys and girls.

Make paper dolls to represent historical characters connected with special holidays: George Washington crossing the Delaware, Abraham Lincoln at Gettysburg, Betsy Ross and the first flag, Grandma preparing Thanksgiving dinner, goblins and ghosts hiding behind real jack-o'-lanterns, or the ringing of the Liberty Bell. And of course at Christmas, your classroom might have a Santa Claus with a pack full of toys (plenty of dolls) and a family of children asleep in their beds.

The collectors whose foreign dolls are shown in this chapter are all blessed with friends or relatives who either travel or live in foreign countries, from Ethiopia to Hawaii, from London to Thailand. Not one of these dolls is more than 9 inches tall, which is exactly the right size for most doll displays.

One good way to display dolls from around the world is to group them on a table, with a large colored map of the world fastened on the wall in back of them. Pin a ribbon to each doll and thumbtack the other end of the ribbon to the country on the map which the doll represents.

Libraries are always interested in displays similar to those suggested for schools. As an example, the dollhouse described in the text and pictured in the previous chapter spent a month in the showcase of a local library, surrounded by an assortment of small dolls busily making a garden. The exhibit was a reminder that the library also had books available on planting flowers and vegetables, as well as on collecting dolls.

A favorite project for girls' clubs or craft groups is to put on a doll show. Every member brings her favorite dolls, and prizes are given for the biggest, the smallest, the prettiest, the homeliest, and the most unusual. This event could be run in connection with a PTA carnival, a church bazaar, or a school open-house.

Once a year, many Scout and Campfire groups are allowed to put displays in their hometown store windows. What could be better than dolls in uniform demonstrating activities and rituals?

And speaking of window displays, your group could dress a wedding party of dolls and offer to let a friendly jeweler use it as his June display, to attract buyers of engagement and wedding rings.

Life-size baby dolls, playing with stuffed toys for small children, could be the center of attraction in a children's-shop window. Large rag dolls would be best for this if they could also be wearing real baby clothes from the shop's regular stock.

One of the oldest uses for dolls was in European nativity scenes at Christmas, a custom that's still observed. The size of the figures ranges from table-top miniatures to life-size replicas dressed in real clothes. You can use dolls you already have and dress them to represent the Holy Family, the shepherds, and the Wise Men. Or you can make dolls from cloth, papier mâché, or wood. Famous religious paintings will give you a good idea of how to dress the figures. The animals should be scaled in the proper proportion to the dolls. Buy them, or make them too. Manger and stable can be built of balsa wood, painted with tempera. Use sand and small pebbles to cover the ground, and put a few trees in the background. It's simple to glue small chunks of plastic sponge, dyed green, to short twigs. Hold the trees upright with wads of clay.

Another good Christmas idea is to make a group of carolers. Sprinkle artificial snow or powdered soap over the ground and on the branches of the make-believe trees. Dress the dolls warmly in caps, scarves, and coats, and put tiny sheets of music in their hands. Place them in front of a small screen that's painted to look like the front of a house. Cut windows in the screen, and behind it hang an electric light on an extension cord. It's easy to imagine the dolls are real little people.

Another way to share your dolls is to make small doll favors for parties. Dress the dolls according to the theme of the party, as folk dancers, football players, bridesmaids, travelers, or babies.

Dolls are interesting additions to special table decorations. Try using an apple-head doll with an arrangement of red apples and autumn leaves. Or prop a clown doll in the center of the table, and tie a string of real balloons to his rag hand. He'll be the most popular guest at a birthday party.

A favorite project for girls' clubs is to make tray favors for hospitals and convalescent homes. Turn pencils into dolls by slipping the eraser end into a doubled circle of paper marked with hair, eyes, nose and mouth. Cover the rest of the pencil with frilled, pastel-colored crepe-paper skirts. The dolls will stand alone.

Another tray favor can be made by marking features on the back of the bowl of a plastic spoon and dressing the rest of the spoon with crepe paper and ribbon. Laid on the serving trays, dolls like these will appeal to both woman and girl patients.

For boy and man patients, how about making gingerbread boys out of cooky dough? You can call them cookies instead of dolls, and not offend their dignity. Decorate the cookies in a tailored way with absolutely no frills, perhaps just a necktie and two or three coat buttons made of icing, with the rest of the costume left to the imagination.

As we come to the end of this story about doll collecting, I'd just like to remind you that it's only the introduction to a subject older than recorded history and as wide as the earth. No one person has ever written it in full or ever can. But it's a hobby full of surprises and delight. It's fact and legend. It will never end. Best of all is the opportunity to join the friendliest group of people in the world — doll collectors.

BIBLIOGRAHPY

Ackley, Edith Flack, *Dolls to Make For Fun and Profit*. Philadelphia-New York: J. B. Lippincott Co., 1938.

————, *Paper Dolls: Their History and How to Make Them*. New York: J. B. Lippincott Co., 1939.

Christopher, Catherine, *Complete Book of Doll Making and Collecting*. New York: Greystone Press, 1949.

Eldridge, Charlotte Blakley, *Godey Lady Doll*. New York: Hastings House, 1953.

Fawcett, Clara Hallard, *Dolls — A Guide for Collectors*. New York: H. L. Lindquist Publications, 1947.

————, *On Making, Mending and Dressing Dolls*. New York: H. L. Lindquist Publication, 1949.

————, *Paper Dolls: A Guide to Costume*. New York: H. L. Lindquist Publications, 1951.

Field, Rachel, *Hitty—Her First Hundred Years*. New York: The Macmillan Co., 1941.

Fletcher, Helen Jill, *See and Do Book of Dolls and Doll Houses*. New York: H. S. Stuttman Co., 1959.

Freeman, Ruth Sunderlin, *American Dolls*. Watkins Glen, N. Y: Century House, Inc., 1952.

Jacobs, Flora Gill, *A History of Doll Houses*. New York: Charles Scribner's Sons, 1953.

Johl, Janet Pagter, *Your Dolls and Mine*. New York: H. L. Lindquist Publications, 1952.

Jordan, Nina R., *American Costume Dolls*. New York: Harcourt, Brace & Co., 1941.

————, *Homemade Dolls in Foreign Dress*. New York: Harcourt, Brace & Co., 1939.

King, Edna Knowles, *A Doll's Family Album*. Chicago: Albert Whitman & Co., 1937.

St. George, Eleanor, *Old Dolls*. New York: M. Barrows & Co., Inc., 1950.

————, *The Dolls of Yesterday*. New York: Charles Scribner's Sons, 1948.

Von Boehn, Max, *Dolls and Puppets,* revised ed. Boston: Charles T. Branford Co., 1956.

INDEX

127

The Author

Helen Young is a newspaperwoman who enjoys two added skills, ceramics and photography. She is the author of an earlier book, Here Is Your Hobby: CERAMICS. For a dozen years she augmented her income by designing and making ceramic dolls and lately has been a regular contributor of how-to articles to *Ceramics Monthly* magazine.